Wh

THE AWESOME ONE isn't meant to just be a motivational quick read. It is a life guide to be used continually as a reminder to rely on Jesus, who is The Awesome One. Amber connects real life examples with scripture to illustrate its relevance to daily living. I love that the book's focus is on personal identity because when you know that you are a child of God, that you belong to Him, then you can confidently walk through life in the grace and love that our God intends for us.

-MATT BEASLEY, eGroup director of Elevation Church, Uptown Campus

THE AWESOME ONE is an invitation for those who are looking for more of God. Amber takes you on a journey of discovering how knowing Him means knowing yourself more and falling deeper in love with The Awesome One. This book meets you wherever you are, no matter the season of life, and is real, raw, and pairs well with an extra shot of espresso.

-MELISSA NEAL, co-founder and senior leader of Generation One Church

Amber's book gives you real life circumstances that you can relate to your own Christian life. You can read this and have references to Biblical scriptures that back up how God uses and teaches us in our own experiences. *THE AWESOME ONE* is a great spiritual reference for any new believer or one that has been a Christian for many years.

-BRIAN BARTH, *Forty Days* band member

This book is a must read! We live in a day and age where we need real, raw, unfiltered truth about who we are and even more so, who God is. *THE AWESOME ONE* is just that; it's authentic, relevant, and packed full of essential truths that every believer needs tucked inside their arsenal for daily living. *THE AWESOME ONE* will be one of my go-to books for years to come.

> -DIANNE WYPER, worship leader and author of *Shattered*

Whether you are struggling to know God or just needing a refreshing reminder of His love, *THE AWESOME ONE* is for you. Through real life stories and solid Biblical truth, it is clear Amber's yearning is for her readers to push past simply acknowledging God but intimately knowing Him! So, sit down, grab a cup of coffee and be ready to laugh, to cry, and to be refreshed as you sit face to face with our God, The Awesome One.

> -NATASHA TUBBS, MDiv., MA., BCCC. speaker and author of *In Pursuit of Purpose*

Amber's book makes you feel like you are in a coffee shop with your best friend discussing how to know God more and grasp the wonderful gift of His grace. *THE AWESOME ONE* will challenge and encourage you in your Christian walk, whether you are brand-new to the faith or have been saved most of your life. She does a great job at diving deep into the message of God's grace and painting it clearly for all to understand.

> -JESSICA PRUKNER, national speaker

Amber's love for God and His word is contagious, and her passion flows through each word that is written. You're going to be inspired and reminded of the overwhelming grace and love of God. This book is full of words that bring hope and truth to the deepest part of your soul.

-JENNY BROWN, founder of Dutton Farm, INC.

Curled up on the couch, I made a plan to read for a little bit before bed. Before I knew it, I had been reading this book for two hours! I grew up in the church my entire life and was amazed at the depth and insight this book offered. I loved that at the end of each chapter, there was a song and reflection questions! You could open any page of *THE AWESOME ONE* and your perspective of God and life would be radically changed for the day ahead!

-JENNA SCHNEIDER, health and wellness coach, wife of Josh Schneider, national speaker and author of *Generation NEXT LEVEL*

I love the encouragement Amber offers you in this book, to dig deeper into your relationship with God through scripture, worship, and reflection. Through wit and widom, *THE AWESOME ONE* gave me all the tools I needed to grow in my faith.

- LIZ FOSTER, non-profit leader

THE
AWESOME
ONE

Unearth who you are by knowing who He is

AMBER OLAFSSON

UNITED HOUSE

For Drew, Emma, and Jack. May you always make knowing God more deeply and sharing about His goodness the goal of your lives. I love you, I am proud of you, and I can't wait to see how God uses you.

READER'S GUIDE

Hey guys! I am so glad you decided to pick up *THE AWESOME ONE*. But hold on, before you get started can I say a quick something? This isn't meant to be a book you start and finish in one day or in a single sitting. Can it be read quickly? Most definitely! Do I advise it? Nope. This suggestion isn't meant to hinder anyone's reading goals for the month, so let me share the heart behind why I hope you peruse through this book gradually. These words have greater purpose than gaining knowledge and are designed to be taken in slowly, so dig in and stay awhile.

THE AWESOME ONE is more than a book, it is a journey to knowing the Lord more deeply than ever before. The words you'll find in the following pages are meant to awaken wonder in your soul and lead you to a real encounter with the living God.

As you read through each chapter, you're going to find lots and lots of scripture. Now, I'm going to shoot straight with you. When I used to read Christian books and the author shared a Bible verse that I'd read and heard a thousand times, I used to instantly think, *Well, I can skip reading this because I already know every word of this verse.* Can anyone relate? If you can, I'm going to ask you a small favor. This time, in *this* book, would you consider reading each verse word for word? I know, I know, I just openly admitted I too have skipped over familiar verses in books, but I am trying to change, and I'm now a recovering verse-skipper. I make this request, because if we really believe the Word of God is alive and active, then every time—every single time—we read a verse, He has the power to reveal something new to us. I hope you'll consider letting God use the Bible verses to speak to you in a fresh way as you read.

You are going to notice that each chapter concludes with a Digging Deeper segment composed of three elements:

- A scripture reference
- A worship song
- A few questions for reflection

Each section will finish with:

- An affirmation to declare

Digging Deeper is meant to be a time where you connect with God.

Invite God into this reading experience with you. Pause at the end of each chapter and do a little digging. See what His Word has to say about the truth shared. Listen to the music and let what you've learned soak in, or spend time simply worshipping our God—the Awesome One Himself. If you are reading this with others, I encourage you to use the questions for group discussion. Lastly, take time to speak the affirmation out loud, reminding yourself who He is and who you are.

Above all, *THE AWESOME ONE* is a tool to help you get to know God more fully. Have an awesome journey with the Awesome One! Enjoy.

CONTENTS

FOREWORD

Have you ever met someone for the first time and immediately knew you were going to be great friends? I'm not talking about the type of friend that comments on the occasional picture of your kids on Facebook. And, I'm not talking about a friend where your conversation with them never exceeds surface level answers to questions like, "How are you?", "How are the kids?", or "What's new?" I'm referring to something different; someone who you knew you were going to do life with. He or she had some quality that was difficult to describe, but you just knew you were meant to be lifelong friends. It might have been their sense of humor, a commonality of interests, or a similar foundation of faith.

Amber Olafsson was a person like that for my wife and I.

In the winter of 2015, we were about to open a brand new, life-giving church in the Metro Detroit area, when Amber and her family stumbled into our doors during our practice service. A practice service is just like it sounds—it's a practice. It's the service before the grand opening. It's the service where none of the volunteers and team members really know what to do or what is going on. There were bound to be many mistakes and miscues during the service. This isn't the service you want any prospective church goer to attend. Even after I explained this to Amber and her husband, they wanted to stay. They told me that they have been waiting for this church to open and felt that this was to be their new church home. I said, "Wait. We haven't even had our first service yet. How do you know this is supposed to be your new church home?" They responded, "We just know this is where God is leading us." Even after all of the miscues and mistakes of our practice service, Amber and her husband were ready to get involved in our new church because they knew God was leading them there.

And that idea is the leading theme in Amber's new book, *THE AWESOME ONE*; that the God who created the entire universe, wants to and is willing to speak to you, lead your life, and use you to make an impact in this world for God. This isn't something reserved for the super spiritual people, pastors or ministry leaders, this is for any Jesus follower. It doesn't matter who you are or what your background is, God has a longing desire to show you who He really is.

As my wife and I began to know Amber more, we

realized that being led by God wasn't something that was just a tag line or bumper sticker motto for her; it was a deep conviction that navigated her life. The more time we spend with Amber, the more inspired we become to seek God with all of our heart, to throw out feelings of shame and inadequacy, and to trust God for things that seem impossible.

In this book, *THE AWESOME ONE*, Amber walks us through her own experiences, her own feelings of failure, doubt, and insecurity and shows us how anyone can establish a firm foundation with Christ and live a life led by the Holy Spirit. She helps us to see how much God truly loves us and that He has a plan for our lives, to make a difference on this earth for Him. Amber's overwhelming desire is to see her readers experience a real and vibrant relationship with the one true God.

That is why I'm so thankful that you're holding this book. I believe God wants to use Amber's life, her story, and her wisdom to help you fall more in love with God than ever before and to be led by Him. As you read, I can assure you that Amber lives what she teaches. She will help you exchange a mindset that screams, "I'm not worthy" or "I'm so unqualified" to the mindset of a God-honoring, world-changing, and Spirit-filled life.

Get ready. It's time to encounter the Awesome One!

Jason & Nicole Rollin
Lead Pastors of City Light Church

3

LET EVERYONE BRING TRIBUTE TO THE AWESOME ONE.

PSALM 76:11B

INTRODUCTION

The call of God often requires us to step out of our comfort zones. When I first felt the tug to write a book about getting to know the Lord of all, part of me was excited, but the other half silently screamed, *"UNQUALIFIED!"* As I considered the task ahead of me, I wrestled with who I was and what qualifications I had for such an undertaking. In my mind, I was not the obvious choice. Ever feel this way? Knowing you've been called to do something, but at the same time, looking over your shoulder and wondering, *'um, did He really mean to ask someone else to do this—because I am not so sure I have what it takes'?*

I was determined to write this book, even though this question frequently popped in my head: *How can I write a book about you, God? I'm no theologian... I'm a stay at home mom for goodness' sake, what do I know?* But, I pushed through the doubt, and three years later, I finished this book about the single most significant treasure in my life: *THE AWESOME ONE*. What I learned through this experience was sometimes we just have to keep walking, showing up, and being obedient despite our feelings of inadequacy. The secret to accomplishing things bigger than ourselves and out of our comfort zones is placing less assurance in our own ability and full confidence in what God is able to do through us.

So, here we are. You are holding the fruit of my unlikely endeavor. The book in your hands is living proof that God doesn't always call the equipped, but He always equips those He calls. This is an ordinary girl's story of how extraordinary God has become to her. He's always been awesome, I just needed to uncover it; when I did, the revelation of who He is became my story and His victory. In the following pages, you will walk through a bit of this journey, and I hope the words penetrate your heart and open your eyes to the possibilities God has for you when you say yes to Him.

Shortly before I answered the call of writing this book, I made the decision to not *just* believe in God and be a Sunday-morning Christian. I wanted more. I wanted to intimately know God as my Father, Jesus as my Savior and King, and the Holy Spirit as my leader, comforter, and empowerer. For me, it was time to go to greater depths in my walk with Him, which has been one awesome ride. He is just too good, I cannot keep Him to myself.

So, grab a cup of coffee (you do drink coffee, right? a.k.a. God's gift to humans—*Thank you Lord!*) and let's start this journey off by taking a deep breath, then exhaling, and relaxing.

First, I'll tell you what this book is not. It isn't full of methods on all that needs to be done in order to get close to God. I will not be sharing a "list every Christian should be checking off daily" or describing how we aren't measuring up. I am tired of books like that and should I come across one, if you are in close proximity you would spot me pitching it across the room.

Okay, seriously though, the main focus of this book is not on *us*, but on *Him*. What I have found to be true is: to know God is to love Him. Yes, I do want us all to become everything we are meant to be (and so does God). But, I'm going to be honest: that doesn't happen by looking to ourselves.

When I zoom in on myself, there always seems to be something I want to change. I start thinking: *I wish I were better at___, When will I stop struggling with___, Will I ever have victory in___, or Why can't I change___?* Often, when I discover a flaw in myself, the immediate response is to focus on it and become consumed with fixing the issue. Now, overcoming and mending problems are good, but I've learned real and lasting change is only achieved by directing the spotlight on the right thing: knowing God and keeping my eyes fixed on Him. The following passage speaks to this:

> *...let us strip off every weight that slows us down, especially the sin that so easily trips us*

up. And let us run with endurance the race God has set before us. **We do this by keeping our eyes on Jesus,** *the champion who initiates and perfects our faith…*

(Hebrews 12:1-2, emphasis added)

We do this: we overcome, we throw off the baggage, we run our race, we become our true selves, we experience freedom from that same old sin, *by* keeping our eyes on Jesus. It is not found in striving harder, following a 3-step method, adhering to religious ceremonies, or by doing more. It is accomplished by placing our full attention on our God: Father, Son, and Spirit. *He* is the key to unlocking the door to the freedom we've been longing for.

I love to see people connect with God, and I want to encourage every reader to dive deeper into His character and *truly* get to know Him. I'm convinced as we experience the love of the One who formed us, our hearts will be ignited with life and purpose. Once we really know Him—when He beckons us to come—we won't hesitate to follow. Because even though we may feel uncomfortable or unqualified for the purpose He has in store for us, we know Him and we trust Him.

One more thing: because this book does not center on us, I have an announcement to make: **the pressure is off!** If this was a movie, God would be the star. Because He is. I am not saying we aren't important—we TOTALLY are—to Him and to His plan in this world. In fact, we bear

His image, we're the bringers of His Kingdom to earth, the children of the Most High, the light of the whole world. We are pretty darn special. But all these attributes we possess are meant to bring Him the ultimate glory. In order to begin seeing our significance, our purpose, and our role in this vast creation, we must first know the Creator. We are going to do just that. By knowing the Awesome One, we unearth who we truly are.

> *Oh, that we might know the LORD! Let us press on to know Him.*
>
> (Hosea 6:3)

ENCOUNTERING THE BURNING ONE IGNITES A BRILLIANT FIRE ON THE INSIDE OF US. AND BECAUSE THIS FLAME DID NOT ORIGINATE FROM THIS WORLD BUT, INSTEAD, IS A SUPER-NATURAL FIRE FORGED IN HEAVEN, IT CANNOT AND WILL NOT BE QUENCHED BY ANY EARTHLY THING. NO DARKNESS, NO FORCE OF EVIL, NO CIRCUMSTANCE, NOTHING CAN PUT OUT THE GLOW OF GOD IN A PERSON'S HEART. IF YOU REACH OUT AND TOUCH THIS HEAVENLY FIRE, YOU WILL SOON FIND YOUR-SELF ABLAZE WITH A POWER UNLIKE ANY OTHER.

ENCOUNTERING
FIRE

I SAW THAT FROM WHAT APPEARED TO BE HIS WAIST UP HE LOOKED LIKE GLOWING METAL, AS IF FULL OF FIRE, AND THAT FROM THERE DOWN HE LOOKED LIKE FIRE; AND BRILLIANT LIGHT SURROUNDED HIM. LIKE THE APPEARANCE OF A RAINBOW IN THE CLOUDS ON A RAINY DAY, SO WAS THE RADIANCE AROUND HIM. THIS WAS THE APPEARANCE OF THE LIKENESS OF THE GLORY OF THE LORD.

EZEKIEL 1:27-28 NIV

1

KNOWING IS GROWING

"I just want to be on fire for God again, like I used to be."
I could hear the ache in my friend's soul as she shared
with me her deepest desire. These words are not uncommon
among followers of Jesus. Either we have said them before,
or we are thinking them now.

It is safe to say that most Christians don't want to
just get by, we actually *want* to mature into people who are
immovable, powerful, and on fire for God. So, we go to
church, we join a small group, we play praise music in our
car, and we read our Bible, but on some days, we still feel
like we need to do more in order to grow. Let's take a look
at what the Bible says about this:

> You will **grow as you learn to know** God better
> *and better.*
> (Colossians 1:10b, emphasis added)

Knowing God produces the growth we're after. It is not more doing but more *knowing*. Many people acknowledge there is a God, but sometimes we can know about something while not having intimate, experiential knowledge of it. I'll give you an example.

I was born and raised in the beautiful state of North Carolina. As a young adult, I thought a change of pace might be nice. So the idea was to move to Michigan for work and then, after a short amount of time, return to sweet home Carolina. With this plan in mind, I embarked on an adventure to the north and promised my family I would never call soda "pop." It wasn't long after my arrival in Michigan that I met my husband, and my agenda for a temporary living situation became an extended relocation. I might as well tell the whole truth, I did start saying, "Pop!" What can I say, it just happened y'all. (Southerners: Don't judge me!)

So there I was, a southern gal living in the north. Basically, I traded sweet tea for hot coffee and flip-flops for snow boots. BIG CHANGE.

Before living in the Mitten State, I thought I knew about the winters—I heard they were harsh and long. Yeah, I didn't have a clue. But now that I have lived through them for 13 years, I KNOW the Michigan winters. I've survived below-freezing temperatures, record breaking snow falls, and learned how to navigate icy roads. I am no longer merely *aware* Michigan has some pretty intense winters, I personally KNOW the crazy that is winter in Michigan. I have experienced it myself, and it ain't no joke.

There is a vast difference in being aware that something exists and actually knowing it personally. This whole book is about us encountering God. Perhaps if we want to "be on fire" for God again, maybe we just need to be with the burning One Himself. I love the passage of scripture from Ezekiel we opened this section with. It pretty much obliterates any image we may have of God being an old man with a white beard. No. This is not what the Awesome One looks like. As described by someone who had a vision of Him, God looks like burning metal, as if full of fire. That sounds pretty magnificent, and He is the awesome treasure we are hunting for. And, you want to know the crazy thing? God actually wants us to know Him. Check out what He says in Hosea:

> ***I want you to know me*** *more than I want burnt offerings.*
>
> (Hosea 6:6b, emphasis added)

We can't miss this; it is His desire. Knowing God is more important than working for Him and sacrificing our time. The Christian life gets real hard, real fast, if we focus more on the rules and neglect the relationship. Actually, it is from a true, healthy, loving relationship with God that we can live a life of excitement with purpose. We're meant to do it with Him.

*Put on your new nature, and be renewed **as you learn to know your Creator** and become like him.*

(Colossians 3:10, emphasis added)

What happens when we encounter our Creator? Life gets awesome because we step into the light of His fire. Knowing God brings renewal and sets our hearts ablaze with fresh passion. We put on our new nature and become like our great God the more we know Him.

Often, we look at the Bible and see a list of requirements on how to live a godly life. And if we're not careful, before we know it, we can find ourselves striving to follow the rules so closely, that we fail to realize that a heart connected to God is what brings the real transformation. People can act right all day long but have hearts far from God, like the Pharisees in the new testament. We will get to the serving, loving, ministering, and doing good. But first, it is crucial we start with the knowing.

I love what theologian J.I. Packer shares about discovering the purpose of life in his book, *Knowing God.*

What were we made for?
To know God.
What aim should we set ourselves in life?
To know God.
What is the "eternal life" that Jesus gives?
Knowledge of God…

What is the best thing in life, bringing more joy, delight and contentment than anything else? Knowledge of God...

What, of all the states God ever sees man in, gives God most pleasure?

Knowledge of himself. [1]

You see, God wants us to know Him more, because He knows what happens as a result of our relationship going to new depths: Hearts burning for Him and set aflame for His Kingdom's cause on the earth. Once we see His heart, it changes ours. What used to be a struggle becomes a delight.

LIVING TREES

There are two kinds of trees: alive and dead. When found in their natural habitat, dead trees are usually rotting, full of pests, and no longer serving their original purpose. Living trees, however, are quite different. When a tree is thriving, it offers shade on a hot day, provides shelter for animals, and (depending on the type of tree) supplies food for consumption, including fruit, syrup, and chocolate (and everybody said Amen!). Trees give and enhance life.

When I started writing this book, I knew I wanted to write about knowing God, so I searched for a theme in order to create imagery in my writing that would help people make a connection. One morning I woke up with an image of a large tree on my mind. At first I thought

RANDOM! Followed by a second thought, *hold on maybe this is significant*. And then it hit me: over and over in the Word of God, strong believers are compared to healthy trees as the prophet Jeremiah shares:

> *But blessed are those who trust in the LORD and have made the LORD their hope and confidence.* **They are like trees** *planted along a riverbank, with roots that reach deep into the water.*
>
> (Jeremiah 17:7-8a, emphasis added)

When I woke up with a tree on my mind, it wasn't random at all. I love the mental picture that likens Christ-followers to mature, established, living trees. It makes me think of the massive oak trees which surrounded the 1800's era farmhouse where I grew up. I have *so* many childhood memories involving those great oaks. I recall twirling in wonder on the tire swing that hung from the lowest branch of the largest tree. After Hurricane Hugo, the limbs scattered across our yard looked like a giant had dropped an entire box of matches. And the time my baby brother climbed a 30-foot ladder leaning against one of the trunks. While he was having the time of his little life, my terrified mom carefully ascended to his rescue. (They both escaped unharmed, if you're wondering—and we got it all on video which makes for a hysterical family movie night.)

A few summers ago, I had the chance to visit my

childhood home. It is now known as the Wings of Eagles Ranch, a non-profit organization that offers therapeutic horseback riding sessions for children and adults with special needs. As I toured the property, I noticed that not all the oaks were still around, but one was, and its leaves were lush, providing much needed shade on that hot day. It was the tree that the tire swing had hung from. The branch which held the swing had broken off, leaving only a short, tattered rope—a tribute to my glorious childhood. What makes a tree grow so firm, to last hundreds of years and still stand strong? Since mature believers are said to "be like trees," it is going to prove vital for us to explore how exactly a tree grows secure. Trees require three basic factors to thrive:

Soil: to sink or anchor their roots.
Light: to fuel growth processes.
Water: to sustain life.

In order for a tree to grow strong and thrive, it needs three basic things: rich soil, sufficient sunlight, and a generous water supply. It's no coincidence there are three key ingredients needed to produce a healthy, vibrant tree, and our Awesome God is comprised of three parts: God the Father, God the Son, and God the Holy Spirit. What if our desire to live purposeful and vibrant lives is found in simply knowing the three persons of God more deeply?

Soil—Know the Love of the Father

Your roots will grow down into God's love and keep you strong.

(Ephesians 3:17b)

Light—Grow in the Light of the Son

I am the light of the world. If you follow me, you won't have to walk in darkness, because you will have the light that leads to life.

(John 8:12)

Water—Overflow with the Life of the Holy Spirit

Anyone who believes in me may come and drink! For the scriptures declare, 'Rivers of living water will flow from his heart.' (When He said "living water," He was speaking of the Spirit, who would be given to everyone believing in him...)

(John 7:38-39a)

Strong, viable growth happens as a result of the right conditions. The difference between surviving and thriving are the conditions in which something lives. As we press in to know our God as Father, Savior, and Spirit, we are set up with the optimal growing conditions. So, let's get ready for powerful growth and purposeful living.

DIGGING DEEPER

Listen to "Build My Life," by Housefires.

Read John 17:3.

1. Think about a time in your life where you have felt most "on fire" or intimately connected to God. How did your life look different than it does now? How does it look similar?

2. How do you experience the soil, light, and water in your life? What do you do to stay rooted in The Father's love, to push yourself forward by the power of Christ, and to let the Holy Spirit move in you?

3. In what areas of your life are you settling for survival when you could be thriving? What can you do to move towards thriving in those areas?

2

OPEN HEART

I recently had a run-in with tar. You know, the sticky stuff they use in road construction. And let me just offer a piece of advice, when it comes to tar ALWAYS assume it's NOT dry—unlike I did. You see, I supposed the black blob beside my porch was hard enough to walk on. Since it appeared dry, I figured *surely* it was but looks can be deceiving, and I quickly discovered it was by no means solid. As the gooey substance engulfed my entire foot, I figured out pretty quickly I had assumed wrong. I went back to my North Carolina roots as the phrase "Tar-Heel" took on a whole new meaning for me. Yuck. Ain't nobody got time for that mess.

Assumptions. They can really mess us up. As we are going on this pursuit of knowing more of God and encountering Him in a fresh way, I suggest we make an accurate assumption: there is ALWAYS more to discover about the Awesome One. In my own journey of pursuing intimacy with the Lord, the closer I get to Him, the more I realize how MUCH there is to learn about this mysterious, wild, good God.

I think preacher Francis Chan hit the nail on the head when he said in his book, *Forgotten God*:

> Is it possible to get enough or even too much God? Is there a point when a person can be satisfied with the amount of intimacy, knowledge, and power of God he or she experiences? I don't see how there can be, because doesn't every encounter with God only cause us to thirst for Him more? Let me be clear. This is not a call to misinformed extremism, but an acknowledgement that as believers we can never be "done" with God. He is infinite and we are finite; there will always be more of His character to discover, more of His love to experience, and more of His power to use for His purposes. [2]

The truth is, I used to assume I had a lot of God figured out. I didn't. A few foundational things, yes. I was a Christian after all. On my faith journey, I have discovered a lot of phrases that I once believed truly described God and the way He thought were actually human-conceived ideals, such as, He's constantly judging me, angry with me all of the time, I'm always in and out of His good graces, He's only happy if I act/dress/speak perfectly—the list goes on and on. Now, if I have a belief about God, I make sure I always have a scripture to back that truth. Every chapter in this book will have a Bible reference, and I encourage you to dig deeper into every topic we hit and find your own verses of promise on the subject.

Over the years, God has exceeded my expectations and blown my mind again and again. In light of this, I have determined to stop putting Him in a box and giving Him limitations in my mind. He is God and I am not. And He can do whatever He wants. (Hello!) So, as I've embarked on writing about Him, I have asked Him to be the teacher. He is the expert on Himself after all, and I am a student who is constantly learning.

I believe if we assume God is going to teach us something new—possibly something we hadn't known or understood before—it will give Him a blank canvas on which to paint a fresh picture in our hearts of our Creator. Let's pray this Psalm together:

> ***Guide me in Your truth and teach me****, for you are God my Savior, and my hope is in you all day long.*
>
> (Psalm 25:5, NIV, emphasis added)

An open, willing, teachable heart gives God SO MUCH to work with. How about we make it our aim to display those qualities when it comes to growing in the things of God? There may be some truths we are still in the dark about, but I believe it is our Creator's intention to bring anything hidden from us out into the light, in His perfect timing. God's Word lights our path, and the truths found there about Him (and ourselves) bring life. Just as healthy trees seek and soak up the sunlight to grow stronger, as we open our hearts and are willing to truly seek God and soak up all He has for us, His light breaks through and produces unbelievable growth.

> *For with you is the fountain of life; in your light*
> *we see light.*
>
> (Psalm 36:9, NIV)

EXPERIENCE IS THE BEST TEACHER

"Don't believe everything you hear," is a common phrase most of us have heard and it is VERY good advice we should all heed. Just because a person had a good or bad experience does not determine how our individual encounter will pan out. Let me give you an example. I used to hear people talk VERY negatively about a local church, and even though this place of worship was reaching people by the thousands, certain church critics were not impressed. Instead of celebrating how many people had turned their lives over to Christ, I constantly heard how "watered down" their sermons were. And, if I am being completely honest, I jumped right on that bandwagon and started saying the same thing about this church.

Until one day I realized those were someone

else's opinions, and all my comments were only adding to division in the body of Christ. I was in no way loving my brothers and sisters. Love covers and hopes for the best, not assumes the worst. So, one day my family decided to check out this "controversial" place of worship for ourselves. And guess what? It was AMAZING. The place was full of life and people were on fire for God. All the junk I heard about this church was completely off. I apologized to Jesus for speaking badly about His body and have tried to never talk negatively about my church "family" again, even if we do have different styles of worship, ways of doing things, or outreach techniques.

Sometimes I think we can get skeptical of God based on other people's stories or opinions of Him. Our experiences with our Creator are going to look different. God made us unique, and therefore, He interacts with people in ways that look different from person to person. Our encounters with Him are going to be as varied as we are. A good rule of thumb is to base your expectation of God on what the Word says, not on what someone else says. If we are going to grow deeper down into God's heart and truly know Him, we have to personally experience Him.

In his book, *Rooted*, Banning Liebscher, pastor of Jesus Culture, shares on the power of experience:

> Intimacy and dependence come only through personal knowledge and encounter. David said, "And those who know your name will put their trust

in You; for You, LORD, have not forsaken those who seek You" (Psalm 9:10). Knowing God's name means knowing Him personally and knowing His nature... God doesn't expect us to build trust in Him blindly, without knowing His character. He doesn't expect us to build trust just on what we've heard about Him. He wants us to build trust on personal knowledge. That's the only way to have true intimacy and dependence.[3]

As we press on to knowing God at a deeper level, my hope is that you will taste and see for yourself that the Lord is good. I am praying whoever finds themselves reading the words of this book will have an unmatched, unforgettable, life-changing encounter with the all-consuming God. I am praying that anyone who opens these pages will have a fresh revelation of our Lord, His character, and His heart. I'm praying as we increase in knowledge of Him, we will equally experience an increase of encounters with Him leaving us all KNOWING there is a God in Heaven who loves us, sees us, and is thrilled to do life with us. He pours holy oil on to us in His presence—like fuel to a flame—and what used to be a spark turns into a heart filled with kingdom fire. When we've been with Him, we are different, and the light He ignites in us shines out. Others will notice and want what we have.

But those who wish to boast should boast in this

> *alone: that they truly know me and understand*
> *that I am the LORD who demonstrates unfailing*
> *love and who brings justice and righteousness*
> *to the earth, and that I delight in these things.*
> *I, the LORD, have spoken!*   (Jeremiah 9:24)

We're allowed to boast? *What?!* Obviously, as the passage makes crystal clear, this is not bragging about ourselves or accomplishments, but truly knowing God is something to be proud of. He wants this for us, and we should want this for ourselves.

Think of your favorite dessert. Now imagine I tried to tell you that your beloved treat was straight up nasty. What if I said, "Nope, you are dead wrong about this dessert being your favorite. That dish is super disgusting!" Would you believe me? Or would you believe your own experience of tasting that deliciousness? Of course, you wouldn't agree with me. You would think my taste buds were dead. And, you would probably say, *"Lady, you are crazy, you need to learn what real food tastes like!"* Well, this is why it is important we don't just believe what others say of God or only read information about Him but actually experience Him in all His glory for ourselves. If and when we have that connection, NO ONE can tell us He doesn't exist, or that He isn't good, or try to convince us with lies about His character. We will know Him on an intimate level, and no one can ever take this away from us.

There are four verses tucked away near the end of

the Bible, penned by the beloved disciple John that I think brings my point home: Experience is paramount for a Christ-follower.

> *We proclaim to you the one who existed from the beginning,* **whom we have heard and seen. We saw him with our own eyes and touched him with our own hands.** *He is the Word of life.* **This one who is life itself was revealed to us, and we have seen him.** *And now we testify and proclaim to you that he is the one who is eternal life. He was with the Father, and then* **he was revealed to us. We proclaim to you what we ourselves have actually seen and heard** *so that you may have fellowship with us. And our fellowship is with the Father and with his Son, Jesus Christ. We are writing these things so that you may fully share our joy.*
>
> (1 John 1:1-4, emphasis added)

My boy, John. Let's do a little recap. This was the only disciple who was at the foot of the cross and there for Jesus during his darkest hour when the other supposedly "devoted disciples" had scattered. This was the guy who outran Peter and reached the tomb to see for himself it was empty. It was John who recognized Jesus before any of the other Apostles when they were fishing and were told to cast their net on the other side by an "assumed stranger." John always seemed to have a spiritual advantage.

John personally knew Jesus. He had not only learned about the Savior of the world, he was intimately connected with the Messiah. Because He was close with Christ and had seen Him, walked with Him, witnessed His miracles, and heard his voice regularly, it turned him into a bold witness. His experience with the Lord positioned him to see things others had not, empowered him to go places others could not, and anointed him to write Holy-Spirit led letters that people all over the world still read over 2000 years later.

From this passage, I see three things that happen as a result of experiencing God on an intimate level:

- We testify and proclaim the goodness of our God without abandon.
- We have a powerful fellowship with the Father, Son, Spirit, and other believers.
- We live a life full of joy the Lord alone gives.

Albert Einstein said, "The only source of knowledge is experience."[4] It is not enough to gather information about God. The only way to know Him is by individually connecting with Him. There is no replacement for time spent in His presence, and there are things we can only receive by being with Him. The great part is the more we are with our awesome God, the more our hearts are molded to look like His, and from this deep fellowship springs unspeakable joy.

DIGGING DEEPER

Listen to "Touch of Heaven," by Hillsong Worship.

Read Ephesians 1:16-17.

1. What is an assumption you made about God's character that He proved wrong the more you got to know Him?

2. What is something you undeniably know about God because of an encounter you had with Him? What did that encounter feel like?

3. How do you connect with God individually? Reflect on your secret place, your pathways, and your access points to Him.

3

GETTING ACQUAINTED

I grew up in an extremely musically-talented family. And by talented, I mean that most of the members of my immediate (and even extended) family can sing, have won singing competitions, professionally sing for a living, and have recorded albums. Or, if they aren't good at singing, they can play instruments. Like, they have MAD SKILLS. Oh, I have uncles, brothers, and cousins who can play any instrument they pick up. They too have albums and YouTube videos that get millions of hits. And can I do any of these things? Nope. How is it that I come from such a harmonious family and the music gene just happened to skip right over me? I got shafted, or so I thought for a long time.

Growing up, I was discouraged that I had no contest-winning abilities. Recently I realized that while I may not be musically inclined, I do have something that does come VERY naturally to me—talking. Now, since almost everyone on the planet possesses this same skill, is it really a talent?

Well, that's beside the point, I need some type of gifting to claim, y'all! My mom will tell you how naturally it came to me, why it even earned me the childhood nickname "the mouth of the south." If that doesn't paint a clear picture, I don't know what will.

So, I do lots of talking, and through this tendency to open my mouth and converse, I've grown to love connecting with people. I am an extrovert, or as my friend Christina recently said, "No, Amber you are an EXTREME extrovert!" This basically means when I am around and chatting with other people, it powers me up. It's so fun meeting new people, and I am constantly growing my old relationships while pursuing new ones, because I just LOVE PEOPLE. I love their stories, I love crying with them and laughing with them and doing life with people from all walks of life.

This love of connection has taught me a few things about developing relationships. If we want to go to a deeper level with anyone, we need to be intentional. Since we're on this pursuit of getting to know God at greater depths than ever before, we have to choose to be all in and really seek Him. With social media and the internet, there are all kinds of unnatural ways to engage with people nowadays (such as seeing what the people we went to high school with twenty years ago eat for dinner every day. That's not normal!), but I'm going to go old school and share a few tried and true keys to healthy relationship building.

In this chapter, we're going talk about a few practical ways to get to know our Creator. I love what God says about this in Jeremiah:

> *If they had stood before me and listened to me,*
> *they would have spoken my words, and they*
> *would have turned my people from their evil*
> *ways and deeds.*
>
> (Jeremiah 23:22)

Don't we all want to speak the words God wants us to say? Don't we all want to turn not only ourselves from evil but also our nations? Being with God is the way we learn how to do this. Engaging in a relationship with our amazing God involves many things, but for this connection to flourish we need to actually be with Him, spend our lives walking alongside Him, and learn to trust Him.

JUST HOLD STILL

My husband and I spent several years overseeing the small groups at City Light Church in Rochester Hills, MI. Since we are always eager to grow, learn new leadership skills, and gain creative ideas to implement in our ministry, our pastor arranged a one-on-one training at Elevation Church in North Carolina for us. This worked out particularly great for our family, because they have locations in and around my hometown. Our kids got to have quality time with Grandpa & Grandma while we had a blast at church, because Elevation is for us what Disney World is for my kids: THE GREATEST PLACE ON EARTH. Every single thing is done with excellence, from the parking lot to the bathroom. No detail is overlooked, and their ministry is so open-handed with their resources and training. The people who attend their churches aren't consumers, they're contributors who radiate the love of God to all. To say they are inspirational would be an understatement.

Okay, moving on from my obvious endorsement and support of Elevation Church (this was not a sponsored statement and full disclosure: when I originally penned these words, I still lived in Michigan, now we are officially North Carolinians and actually attend Elevation, so their investment has come full circle)... back to the story... After an exhilarating morning of behind the scenes set-up, meeting campus, small group, and children's pastors, attending their volunteer training, sitting in on team meetings and watching baptisms, my husband and I got "the dreaded call." You know, the one no parent wants to get. We had only been gone a few hours when my mom called to tell me, "We are on the way to Urgent Care with Drew. He got a toothpick stuck in his foot."

Timeout. At this point you are probably thinking two things: one, *GROSS* and two, *HOW does that even happen?* I know this, because in that moment those were my exact thoughts... But, assuming it wasn't *that* bad, I calmly said, "Ok, mom, you don't have to take him to urgent care. If we were there, Andrew would just get tweezers and pull it out."

After a moment of silence she replied, "Well, the

thing is, we can't see it anymore."

Now, she had my attention, and I got a little more concerned, "What now?"

"It is all the way in," she replied.

Well that changed things.

I took a few seconds to process what I had just been told. After gathering my thoughts, I responded, "Okay. We'll be right there!" We proceeded to cut our training day short and made a mad dash for the closest urgent care.

For those who are curious, the kids were making a craft and a few toothpicks had fallen onto the carpet. My son, who is very active and easily excited, at one point jumped off the chair onto the floor, and his foot collided with the toothpick at just the right angle and, well, the rest is history. #crazystuffhappenswithkids

Drew was extremely brave, but the whole experience was quite traumatic for a 7-year-old. Who am I kidding—this would be traumatic for anyone! He was most worried about the pain from the shot that would numb the incision area. I told him he had to keep his foot very still so they could get the shot in the right place, take away the pain, and be able to clean out the wound so he could heal. It was important he remained still for the procedure so the doctor could get close, be precise, and the damage could be fixed. He was a trooper and held as still as possible while the doctor got him all taken care of. But I think the most important thing Drew learned that day was to never skip church again. I mean, obviously bad things happen when you play hooky on Jesus.

RELAX, I'm kidding!

Since I have three young kids, bumps, bruises, and blood come with the territory, and I deal with a lot of boo boos. Some wounds are worse than others, and occasionally we get one that needs a little more than a kiss from mama. (Like the toothpick fiasco!) If my children don't come to me and sit still, I cannot clean the wound and bandage it properly. Similarly, as God's children, we need to intentionally choose to be still in life and frequently meet with Him so He can do some mending.

Life never stops. We seem to go from one thing to the next, but even though time keeps ticking by, there are endless opportunities to be still. God is always there. Always available. Always waiting. If we never take time to be still and meet with Him, how can He get close? How can we know Him? How can He reveal Himself as our healer? How can He fix what has been hurt? How can He mold our hearts to look like His?

> **Be still, and know** *that I am God!*
> (Psalm 46:10a, emphasis added)

Just as my son needed to remain still and calm so the doctor could do her best work, we too need to intentionally choose to be still in life and frequently meet with God so He can do His best work. The more time you spend with someone, the more you get to know them. Being with God grants Him access to our hearts, where He does life-changing work. Being still lets Him come close. Being still allows us to hear from Him. Being still opens the door for Him to heal our wounds. Perhaps it is in the being, not the doing, that we get to know Him the most. I'll share more on how to "just be" with God in the next few sections.

TAKE A WALK

"I've started jogging," I told my good friend.

"You did WHAT?!" She replied, mouth open, totally in shock. This was big news, because ALL of my close friends know I do not enjoy working out. I have to jog now, because apparently my metabolism decided to not work as great as it used to. What's up with that?

I do, however, have one favorite exercise: Walking. I love it, mostly because it can be enjoyed with another person, and I still have the lung capacity to carry on a conversation. I don't enjoy walking alone. But, I have three children, so I haven't gone on a walk by myself, well, since they were born. Once we have kids we are never alone again, and that includes when visiting the bathroom. What happened to privacy?!

What I enjoy about walking is:

- I feel like I've worked out, but I don't get out of breath or break a sweat (Hallelujah!)
- I get to do it with someone and we can talk. (I think we've covered my extroverted need for

socialization.)

On evenings when the weather is nice, our family heads out to the neighborhood and the kids ride scooters or get pushed in the stroller while my husband and I fill each other in about our days. We leave our phones behind and get to connect distraction-free. It's glorious. My favorite part of walking is the person I'm doing it with—it's the communication we're having. It is enjoying being in the presence of a loved one. Heart filling.

One day I was reading the Bible and a new character grabbed my attention: Enoch. You don't hear too many sermons on this guy. Actually, I have never heard any. He has like five sentences about him in the scriptures (maybe this is why). But, if he was important enough to get in the Bible, I'd say he's worth looking at.

So, Enoch. In Genesis 5:21-24 (NIV) we learn a little bit about the guy.

> *When Enoch had lived 65 years, he became the father of Methuselah. After he became the father of Methuselah, **Enoch walked faithfully with God** 300 years and had other sons and daughters. Altogether, Enoch lived a total of 365 years. Enoch walked faithfully with God; then he was no more, because God took him away.*

His name is referenced in a few other verses speaking of his lineage and saying what we already know… which isn't a whole lot.

Do you know what jumps out at me about him? This simple phrase: Enoch walked with God. Then, God took him to Heaven. I remember reading that the first time and thinking *That's it? This is all we get? I want some more details!!!* But then it hit me. Enoch lived in a time where there was no written Bible (that we know of). At this point in history it all would have been orally passed down, as paper, pens, and the printing press had not been invented. Yet, this guy had a vibrant relationship with God. How? Because he walked with Him. He talked with Him. He did life with God. And, he didn't even read his Bible every day because He couldn't! So, I want to take this moment to say if you miss a day reading the Bible, you are okay! You aren't out of fellowship with God or a bad Christian. Release yourself from that lie. Enoch NEVER read the Bible, and God liked him so much he didn't let him die. *Boom.*

I am not saying we shouldn't read our Bible. Reading the Word is a good thing to do and is essential to growth. The scriptures show us more about God's love and offer us hope. They teach us about our Savior and guide us in truth. Please read the Bible. But, what I am saying is this: if we are having a busy day, a tough season, or life is just non-stop and we don't have even a moment to be in the Word… we can just be with the Word. Be with Jesus. We can be like Enoch and remember the truths about God. We can say them over in our mind. We need to remember we can walk with Him even if we haven't read the Bible in a week, or like ever. *Phew.* Pressure off.

When we walk with someone, we converse, we catch up on life, and talk about our day. We know their voice. We don't run ahead of them or lag behind, we are simply with them. This is how it is supposed to be in our relationship with God. He wants to do life with us—at our side. He wants to be a part of cleaning the house, the drive on the way to work, the decisions we make, and the interactions we have. He doesn't want us running ahead of His plan for us or falling back when He is leading. He wants us in step with all He is doing, taking an active part and staying in constant conversation with Him.

So, what does this look like practically?

- Talking with Him regularly, because prayer at its simplest is just a conversation with God.
- Asking Him questions about big decisions and even the small ones.
- Getting His advice before we respond to others.

Pastor Judah Smith talks about walking with God in his book, *How's Your Soul?*, and shares:

As we spend time with God, we will advance. We will change and improve. But we have to remember that the point of our walk with God is not arriving. The point is walking. The point is being in relationship with God and experiencing life together.[5]

Looking at Enoch reminds me to have a simple relationship with God. We don't need to do a million things to connect with the Creator, we just need to walk with Him. The more we walk with God, the more we will know Him. It doesn't have to be more complicated than that. Keep it simple. Faith like a child.

TRUST ME

House hunting is not for the faint of heart. A few years ago, we were looking for a home for our family. At the time, we were living with relatives; we had moved three times with a newborn in less than a year and it was taking a toll on all of us. We were DONE and oh so ready to find our permanent home. Every house we looked at brought the hope: Okay, maybe *this* is the one. We looked for months. We would offer and get outbid. Every. Single. Time.

Then we found one. It was beautiful, the yard was great, schools were awesome, location was amazing, and so we offered. We prayed about how much to bid on the house and felt God give us "the right" amount. I loved that house and even wrote the owners a note saying how I could just picture myself sitting on the front porch watching my kids ride their bikes in the summer, while drinking my sweet tea. Oh yes, I did. I thought surely that would seal the deal. I was finally allowing myself to get excited! But, they turned down our offer, no counter, just flat out said no. My heart sank. I was so discouraged and questioned God. *I thought you said don't offer any higher? Now this?* All this waiting and we find out what we thought was "it" turned out was not. Can anyone relate?

So, after not getting that much-wanted home, we had to recalibrate. We needed to remind ourselves that the God we serve—the one who loves us—ALWAYS has our best in mind, and we can trust Him. Hope lifted, and again we sought His guidance, surrendering our plans to His.

Well, fast forward a month, and we finally found "the one." As soon as we walked into our last home, we had an unexplainable peace. We just knew. We offered and got accepted that day and the rest is history. I loved the location even better than the other home, I loved the schools, I loved the neighbors, I loved the house. God just knew. Doesn't He always?

Sometimes when an expectation isn't met, we can fall hard. But just because our plan does not pan out the way we had envisioned, does not mean God isn't worthy of our confidence. Even if we get disappointed, angry, or sad, as long as we remember God can be trusted, we can rise with fresh hope. Things not going according to our plans just means He has something else in mind for us. His ways are higher than our ways and He can see things we can't.

*And we know that **in all things God works for***

the good of those who love him, *who have been*
called according to his purpose.

(Romans 8:28, NIV, emphasis added)

Trusting God is a byproduct of knowing Him. Just like any other relationship, the more acquainted we are with a person, the more we learn of his or her character; the end result is a deep and unshakeable trust. As we take time to do life with God and experience a more intimate connection, He begins taking us to new levels of dependence on Him. When we believe He is for us, loves us, and has our best interest in mind, it becomes second nature to have full faith in Him. When we are convinced in all things, even the unmet expectations, God will work it out for OUR good. It builds in us an unshakable confidence in the Lord.

Pastor Rich Wilkerson, Jr. speaks about trusting God in his book, *Sandcastle Kings*:

> The question is not "Do you believe God exists?" or "Do you believe that Jesus is the Son of God?" The question is, "Do you trust God?" Belief is important, but in the darkest days it is trust that gives us hope… Trust goes beyond belief… Religion tells us to believe. Believe this doctrine. Believe these truths. Believe this dogma. But a relationship with Jesus goes beyond mere belief. Relationship requires trust. [6]

Without trust, any relationship is unhealthy. In order for us to get to know God deeper than before, we must choose to open up our hearts to trusting Him completely and allow the all-consuming fire of God to take root in our lives. The more time we dedicate to intentionally walk with Him and know Him, the deeper our confidence will be.

Absolute trust is born out of a fundamental foundation of love, and that is what we'll be looking at next. Because until we know someone loves us, it can be hard to trust them. Love provides safety in relationships and produces a healthy, secure ground where trust can grow.

HE IS GOD, THE AWESOME ONE
I AM CREATED TO KNOW HIM

DIGGING DEEPER

Listen to "I Want To Know You," by Jesus Culture.

Read Jeremiah 29:12-14.

1. Do you find it difficult to be still before God, or is it something that comes naturally to you? What can you do practically to ensure you have moments of pause with Him?

2. How can you invite God into your everyday tasks like driving, cleaning, and interacting with others?

3. What is an experience in your life where your expectations were not met like you hoped they would be? Can you point out where God was in that situation? How have you seen Him work it for your good?

THERE IS AN UNSTOPPABLE FORCE THAT RIPS THROUGH CHAINS, PRIES OFF PRISON DOORS, AND SETS CAPTIVES FREE. WHAT HAS THE UNMATCHED STRENGTH TO DO THAT? LOVE. AND NOT JUST ANY LOVE. GOD'S LOVE. A PREVAILING LOVE. A DYNAMITE LOVE. THIS IS A LOVE THAT DOESN'T BLAST PEOPLE TO KINGDOM COME, BUT SPARKS A REVOLUTION AND ROLLS OUT THE WELCOME MAT FOR GOD'S KINGDOM TO COME. THE WORLD NEEDS TO EXPERIENCE THE EXPLOSIVE POWER OF GOD THE FATHER'S LOVE.

DYNAMITE LOVE

MAY YOU HAVE THE POWER TO
UNDERSTAND, AS ALL GOD'S PEOPLE
SHOULD, HOW WIDE, HOW LONG, HOW
HIGH, AND HOW DEEP HIS LOVE IS.

EPHESIANS 3:18

4

A STRONG FOUNDATION

The steaming, black coffee tasted glorious as I enjoyed every sip during my quiet time that morning. Coffee and Jesus is the best combo. *Can I get an Amen?* There was nothing out of the ordinary about this morning. Everything happened like it always did: husband off to work, one kiddo off to preschool, and the other one was plopped in front of the TV for a little educational show (so mama could read the Bible peacefully for 15 minutes — you gotta do what you gotta do). But something extraordinary was about to happen.

I found myself reading through 1 John 4 in the New International Version and I came to verse 20, which goes a little something like this:

> *Whoever claims to love God yet hates a brother or sister is a liar. For whoever does not love their brother and sister, whom they have seen, cannot love God, whom they have not seen.*

I read the verse casually and in all honesty my first thought was, *A Liar? Well, tell me what you really think, John!* And my second, *I do like my brothers and all my family, so I'm good there,* I reasoned confidently.

This was when another voice interrupted my thoughts, *No, you don't.* I had heard it often enough to know who would be so bold as to interrupt my Jesus time: it was God himself.

And so, the conversation with the Holy Spirit started.

Me: *What do you mean I don't love my brothers and sisters? Of course I do.*

HS: *You love your physical family, yes. But, not your spiritual family. You see, everyone who calls on Jesus as their Savior has the same Father you do, and that makes them your brother and sister.*

Me: *Oh shoot.*

He had me there. Suddenly, I was flooded with memories of Christians who had hurt me: churches, ministries, and speakers who I didn't agree with on every single theological point. Not only did I not love them, I also realized there was a good chance I had talked negatively about their style of worship or methods. In a split second, I had a revelation that my spiritual family went way beyond my home and the walls of my own personal church community. As I hit the brick wall of reality, my eyes were opened. I did not, in fact, love my brothers and sisters in Christ.

I relented. *Ok, God. You're right. How do I get*

there? Show me how to love. This started me on a journey of a lifetime, a quest for real love, and I have never looked back.

First, God called me *out* on love, then He called me *up.* He showed me where I was, then He lifted me and gave me a heavenly perspective of people. He patiently walked with me and worked with me to demonstrate the power of His love and what it can do to a human heart. And although I was a die-hard Christ follower before, I had a calloused heart which needed to undergo a restoration to its original function: a soul that unconditionally loves all people.

> The impulse of a converted soul is to love, and not to be getting up and complaining of everyone else and finding fault. [7]

Somebody preach! Evangelist D.L. Moody said this over 100 years ago, and it is still just as true as ever. I'll be the first to tell you I used to be a part of the latter. I could find fault with the best of them, but God showed me a better way: His way. I found being negative and finding fault in others is a prison, and GOD'S LOVE, well it's a jail breaker. As I walked this love-journey, I experienced an explosion which decimated the bars confining my heart and set me free. My hope is that this same dynamite-power love of God would detonate in all His sons and daughters, setting souls free, resulting in a people who love without abandon and are an unstoppable force who radiate the love of God to all the world.

FLAT BROKE

They say when you have young kids going to the grocery store alone is like a vacation. Well, I wasn't on vacation *that* day. I decided that making a grocery run with all three of my children was a good idea. First mistake.

We had made it all the way through the store with lots of "No, we can't get that. Please stop pushing each other. For the love, put that back!" It is always an adventure. I was now at the checkout with a cart full of groceries and somehow thought self-checkout would be faster. Yeah right. What was I thinking? After allowing the kids to take turns scanning items, calming fits of laughter and confiscating candy swiped by the baby (the struggle is real) I FINALLY had all my items bagged.

I ran my check card through to pay, and for the first time in my life, I got the error code: DECLINED.

I thought, *What? Well that has to be a mistake.* I swiped it again, same message. After a third try I called over an attendant, because *surely* the machine was broken. We tried debit & credit. Nothing worked. I tried calling my husband. No answer.

Of course, by this time I am totally a wreck. Shocked, embarrassed, and sweating like nobody's business, I have no other choice but to abandon all the groceries and leave the store, mortified. What happened was our mortgage payment was taken out earlier than scheduled. So, there was in fact no money in the account. At that moment, I was flat broke. And no matter how much I wanted to buy those groceries and come home with a trunk full of food, it wasn't happening. If I wanted to spend money, I needed to have money. We got it all worked out, but it's not an experience I EVER want to relive.

Trying to spend money I didn't have—that is how I would explain the way I used to live my life as a Christ-follower. I was attempting to love others and God with a love I didn't comprehend or personally know. I wanted to love well and I knew I should be doing so, because it is, after all, the greatest commandment according to Jesus. But, I always felt like I wasn't loving Him or others enough. I constantly evaluated my spiritual condition on my love: *How well am I loving?* And when I took an honest look at myself, I was falling short.

But I had it wrong. Not the commandment to love— that is right. Christians should absolutely be loving well. What I had wrong was the how: how to *actually* love well. I strived to love others because I was commanded to, but I had no power to actually walk it out. I had always tried to follow the rule, but without a heart change. Essentially, I was trying to write a check without making a deposit. It doesn't work that way. We can't buy something for cash if we don't have the money. We can try, but we are not going to get very far. In the same way, no matter how much I wanted to love well I couldn't consistently do it. Because if I wanted to show love, I first needed to receive that love on the inside of me, and I had to get it from the only true source: God.

Oh sure, I knew God loved me. Most Christians believe the song lyrics, "Jesus loves me." We're taught it from birth. But knowing "He loves me" was only in my head, not in my heart.

> *I want you to show love*, *not offer sacrifices.*
> *I want you to know me more* *than I want*
> *burnt offerings.*
> (Hosea 6:6, emphasis added)

I believe there is a connection in knowing God and showing love. I don't mean knowing *about* Him, I'm talking about truly knowing our great Creator on an intimate level. I love how pastor Joseph Prince explains this:

> God wants you not just to have head knowledge of His Love, but also to believe in and *taste* His love for yourself. It can't just remain in your mind or in the cerebral realm of logic; it has to be experienced in your heart. Today, believe with all your heart that God loves you. No matter how many mistakes you have made, He has not given up on you! He is for you. The first key to right believing is to believe in His unconditional love for you.[8]

God wants a genuine relationship with us, and His desire is that we love Him and others extravagantly.

By knowing God intimately and experiencing His love personally, we are thrust into a life of showing love, supernaturally. Let's lean in, press on to know the love of God, and receive a deposit of heavenly love in our hearts so we can display this love.

DADDY ISSUES

Just hold it together, DO NOT cry or you will mess up all your makeup. I thought as I tried, in vain, to hold back the tears streaming down my face as my dad sang to me at my wedding. Every word was a like a precious blessing composed into a beautiful "send-off" to my new married life.

Dads. They sure leave an impact. A father is one of the most significant role models in our life, and their influence, or lack thereof, will go way beyond our time spent with them. A dad's love plays a huge part in our confidence, security, and our need for approval. I've heard it said that our experience with our earthly father will have a huge impact on how we interact with our Heavenly Father. If we've had a good relationship with our dad, usually we are open to God as Father. If our earthly dad treated us insignificantly, it can be difficult to believe God the Father can be trusted or find anything special about us. Or, there is this third category, the one I fit into. Since my dad and father-in-law are both great, I was absolutely open to God as Father, but because I had good father figures, it was difficult for me to see a need for another one. He was my God, but not really my dad. I naively thought I had this covered. I will show you what I mean.

First, there is my biological father, Tim, whom I affectionately call "Daddy." He is the one who was dead set on my middle name being "Grace;" for him there was no other option. I'm thankful for the resolve he had, because learning of God's grace—this almost-sounds-too-good-to-be-true gospel—changed my life. He has always been my biggest fan and never missed a single one of my sports games growing up. My daddy is a magnificent singer and songwriter and even composed the song he sang at my wedding. I first heard the words of "Amber's Song," just before he gave me away at the altar. And let's just say I was thankful I had on waterproof mascara that day. He is a good, constant, calm dad.

Then there is Thor—yes that is his real name, and can I just say right now: How cool is it that I have a superhero for a Dad?! Don't be jealous. Alright, all jokes aside, this is my husband's dad and he is descended from the Vikings (my boys in particular love this little factoid about our heritage). His father was an immigrant from Iceland—came right through Ellis Island and everything. He is the one who gave me my Scandinavian last name—Olafsson—which hardly anyone can pronounce and no one can spell right on the first try. But, I love it. He became my second dad back in 2005 when I married into this great family. Thor, also known as Bud, is a builder by trade and competes in Marathons to raise money for Hope Water International's mission to provide clean water in Africa. He has always welcomed me with open arms and treated me like his own daughter. Thor is also the reason I have started jogging and why I'm a bit of a coffee fanatic—he's the one who instructed me to always drink it black—um, is there any other way? He is kind, loving, friendly, and a great encourager.

Yes, I have two great earthly dads. But as awesome, consistent, loving, and caring as they are, my relationship with them was never meant to trump my connection with my Father in heaven. His love is unmatched, essential, and irreplaceable. So, if we had an amazing dad(s) in our life, that is fantastic—they've paved the way for us to be open to God as our Father. He is going to take it from there and be our ultimate Dad. Because as great as they are (or were), they could never supersede the perfect love of a Heavenly Father, and they were never meant to. There is literally NOTHING like His love.

But, what if we've had a bad impression of a dad? Maybe he wasn't around, didn't value us, withheld love, only approved when we acted "good," was abusive, or didn't even glance our way? First, if you can relate to that kind of relationship with a father, I am sorry. You deserve better because you are worthy of love and approval. God never intended a father-child relationship to be marked by pain.

Maybe your earthly dad wasn't great, and he hurt you, leaving a gaping hole in your heart you are not sure will ever heal. I am here to tell you God is not capable of causing that kind of pain. He is the perfect Father, who has come to mend your wounds completely and restore all that was lost. His love for you is great, He sees you, and is fed up with the enemy stealing away your life. I want to share a few powerful sentences from the book *Captivating*:

> God has sent me on a mission.
> I have some great news for you.
> God has sent me to restore and release something.
> And that something is you.
> I am here to give you back your heart and set you free.
> I am furious at the enemy who did this to you, and I will fight against him.
> Let me comfort you.
> For, dear one, I will bestow beauty upon you where you have only known devastation.
> Joy, in places of your deep sorrow.
> And I will robe your heart with thankful praise in exchange for your resignation and despair.[9]

We have a Father who loves us, and while the same may or may not be true of our earthly fathers, it is most certainly true of our heavenly Father.

Whether we have been hurt by our earthly father or had a charming childhood, this need to receive His love exists for all of us.

When we choose to let Him in, and the Holy Spirit fills our hearts with the prevailing love of Almighty God, we begin to see our earthly dads in a new light. We discharge them from having any negative effect on us. We are complete in the love of our Heavenly Father. I found letting God take the lead role as Father in my life gave me the ability to release my earthly dads from having to be perfect.

I am living proof you can go to church, volunteer faithfully, lead ministries, be saved and on your way to Heaven, but not fully grasp what it means to have God as a Father. To me He was Lord, not dad. Until God became my dad, I didn't really act like His child. Oh, I was serving Him alright, like a servant waits on His master—completely devoted to His commands, but half afraid of what He would do if I messed up. That is not a healthy relationship. It wasn't that *He* ever gave me this impression, religion did. I was SUPER religious and did not really interact with Him on a relational level. I knew His rules, but I struggled to follow them. But then something magnificent happened: I opened up my heart to Him teaching me about His true love and, like a dad holding his daughter's hand, He patiently walked with me through the learning process. He showed me that love was the starting place for any effective ministry.

For you did not receive a spirit of slavery to fall back into fear. Instead, you received the Spirit of adoption, by whom we cry out, "Abba, Father!"

*The Spirit Himself testifies together with our
spirit that we are God's children…*
(Romans 8:15-16, CSB)

I had been a Christian in need of a love lesson. Jesus
was my Savior, but I was far from following His example
in the way He treated people. He was able to love the
unlovable, because He knew God as Dad, and He knew He
was His beloved son. His public ministry on earth started
with a reminder:

> *When Jesus was baptized, he went up
> immediately from the water. The heavens
> suddenly opened for him, and he saw the Spirit
> of God descending like a dove and coming down
> on him. And a voice from heaven said: "This is
> my beloved Son, with whom I am well-pleased."*
> (Matthew 3:16-17, CSB)

Essentially, God the Father says, "I'm His dad and
I love Him." God affirmed his identity and love for him,
and then Jesus got to work. It is the same for us. When I
surrendered my trapped heart to the work of the Holy Spirit,
He ripped the jail door open and filled that space with
Himself. God's love invaded my soul, and then I started
calling Him my Daddy in Heaven. I stepped into the position
He always intended for me, and my true calling: a daughter
of God.

So now, I have one more dad to tell you about: my Father in Heaven, the Awesome One. He's the perfect dad, the one who formed me, picked out my eye color, chose the pigmentation of my skin, and decided what family I would fit into. He designed my personality and gave me talents to bring Him glory. He is the one who has had His hand on me my whole life and has been my confidence since youth. He's good, patient, gracious, faithful, wise, and always has time for me. I'm still mining the depths of His character, and each day I unearth new gems about Him. I think I always will. But His love, there is nothing like it in this world. When He showed me how much He loved me, it woke me up and changed the trajectory of my life. Experiencing His lavish love awakened me to my true self.

HAVE YOU HEARD?

A lot of people have reputations that precede them. Sometimes we hear good things and look forward to meeting this particular person, and sometimes we hear the not-so-good things and hope our paths never cross. Have you ever heard stories about someone and thought: *Wow, I want to be friends with them?* This actually happened to me a few years ago.

My family attended City Light Church from the day they opened their doors (Well, technically the week before they officially opened them; remember the story from the foreword?) until the week we moved to North Carolina in

2017. I love that place, my City Light Church family, the pastors, and boy was it hard to leave. One day shortly after we had been attending, Pastor Jason said, "Hey Amber. I've got someone you need to meet. Her name is Charity, and she lives in the same city you do. She's new to the area, has four children who are around your kids ages. She's SUPER sweet, and I don't know, I just think you two would get along."

I was like, "Point her out now!" However, I had to wait to meet her as she wasn't there that Sunday.

A few weeks went by, and I still had not met Charity. But, after Pastor Jason mentioned her to me, I heard about her in various conversations with various people. I was excited to finally connect with Charity. (Fun little fact about me, I love meeting new people—always have.)

One day I was working at the church information table, and a lady approached me followed by a bunch of kids. She was smiling and said, "Are you Amber?"

I replied, "Are you Charity?" We started chatting and connected right away. We had both heard about the other but had not officially met until that moment. Shortly afterwards, I had her over for coffee (because that's what I do when I want to get to know someone), and we quickly discovered we were kindred spirits. Charity loves worship music, loves spending time at the feet of Jesus, and loves coffee—I mean how much more perfect can a friend be?!

Charity became one of my closest friends, and she still is to this day. She played a huge role in this book being published. She believed in me as a writer, helped me name my last book, and even brainstormed with me on songs, chapter titles, and the tagline for this book. She has been a huge supporter of my dream of becoming a publisher and was the first one to join my publishing team.

When I heard about her years ago, I had no idea who she was, but I wanted to get to know her more. At first, I *knew about* Charity, but now, I *know* Charity, and I am thankful that I do!

In this digital age we live in, it is easy to learn a lot about a person extremely quickly. We can jump on Google, Instagram, or Facebook and gather information or pictures really fast. However, hearing or reading about someone does not necessarily mean we know them or are known by them (especially since social media rarely reveals the whole truth). Take God for instance. The Bible tells us He loves us. So, that is some information we've heard about Him. But knowing that God loves everyone and knowing God's love for us personally are two different things. To live an explosive life filled with love we must go beyond "hearing about" God's love and truly come to know the unique love He has for each one of us. It must become our own.

We know how much God loves us, and we have put our trust in his love. **God is love, and all who live in love live in God, and God lives in them.**

(1 John 4:16, emphasis added)

In order to "live in love" we must have a firsthand experience with supernatural love. When we know how much we're loved, it takes us to a whole new level of trust in our relationship with our "Daddy" in heaven. Grasping God's individual love for us is an essential part of establishing our foundation as Christ-followers. I'm married to a builder, so I know if there is a crack in the foundation, it is going to negatively affect the entire house. Meaning, if one key element is off, everything else will be too. Knowing we are treasured by the Creator of the universe sets us up to live powerfully and positions us to stand firm. Pastor Judah Smith shares what grasping God's out-of-this-world love will lead to in one of his recent books, *Life Is ____*.

> Life is to be loved and to love. The order of those two phrases is intentional, because until we realize we are loved, it's tough—probably impossible—to truly love... the love that matters most, the love that enables us to know we are valuable and significant, is God's love for us... I am convinced that's the main message of the entire Bible. *God loves you.* Once we begin to grasp his love, it's a lot easier to love other people. There is something about God's love that helps us look past ourselves and see those around us. Life is meant to be lived in love.[10]

We know we're supposed to follow after God's ways and love like He does. As we allow ourselves to accept His love for us, we will do just that. As our roots are strengthened in His love, our ability to love others will stretch—like a tree's branches that offer abundant shade—wider than we ever thought possible.

> ***Follow God's example, therefore, as dearly loved children,*** *and walk in the way of love…*
> (Ephesians 5:1-2a, NIV, emphasis added)

When we see ourselves as the dearly loved children of God we *will* follow His example. We are created in His image and He has a heart full of love towards us. We have to live every moment fully aware we are extravagantly, over the top, SO loved, not because of what we've done, but because of who we are: God's beloved sons and daughters. Again, it is one thing to hear that you are beloved and quite another thing to walk in light of that truth. When we know Him as a loving Father, when we meet our good God, who is love itself, we are forever changed. Because love changes everything.

DIGGING DEEPER

Listen to "Good Good Father," by Housefires.

Read John 17:26.

1. Think about people in your life who you naturally show love to, and then think about others you may have to work to love. Why do you think that is?

2. How has your experience been with earthly father figures? In what ways have they helped you better understand the Father Heart of God? In what ways do you still need connection with Him as Father?

3. How has the love of God changed you? In what ways does your life look different because of God's love for you?

5

FILLED UP

I grew up babysitting. Once, I babysat for a weekend and let me tell you I hit the jackpot. It was not my typical gig where I got twenty dollars for a night, this time I got paid seventy-five bucks! That was a lot for a young girl—I thought so anyway. Well, do you know what happened? After getting paid, I lost that check. When the parents noticed the funds never left their account, they asked me if I misplaced it and needed them to cut me a new check, and I lied. I was too embarrassed to tell them the truth. I covered by saying, "No, I am just waiting to cash it." Oh, I waited alright. I'm still waiting. I never found that seventy-five-dollar check. So, even though I had ALL this money, I never got to use it. Shame kept me from going to the source for more.

Ever since the lost check fiasco, when it is payday, the first stop I make is the bank where I deposit the check right away. I attempt to leave no room for error. My goal is to get that baby to safety or who knows where it will end up. I am happy to report, however, that even though recently one of my checks ended up in the wash and was utterly destroyed, I did fess up to the person who gave it to me, and I got a new one. Now, if I could just learn to empty my pockets! #babysteps

Now let's talk about a spiritual payday, which means much more than a physical paycheck. Only this payment was not and cannot be earned. I'm speaking of the unconditional, unearned love of God that is available for each and every one of us. And, if we can push past our insecurities, shame, and lies of the enemy, we can approach the source of all love and receive a much-needed payday for our souls.

To walk out a lifestyle of love, we first need a deposit made into our hearts of the unmatched love of God. Christianity is about Him loving us first, way before we ever get to us loving others well. If we get that order reversed, the task of loving people seems hopeless and downright impossible. But, if we do this thing right, if we first receive, *then* give, our love will be unstoppable.

If we want people to be able to say of us, "I know they are Christians by how they love people," we must first become the beloved of our Heavenly Father. Just as "a hurt person hurts people," "a loved person loves people." When that happens, when we personally encounter His love, that great commandment to love God and others—that we all want to follow so badly—becomes less an instruction and more a reaction. It's meant to be walked out as an overflow from the heart of a person who is loved. We can't help loving once we are truly loved; it becomes who we are and what we do.

*We love each other **because** he loved us first.*
(1 John 4:19, emphasis added)

Just like we have to get paid before we can start spending money, we need to know His love before we can start loving. Previously, that had been my problem. I had it backwards. My love account had been empty. I was fixed on my own ability to love, when all along that wasn't going to solve anything. The solution lay with knowing God, connecting to His love, and embracing the fact that I was (and am) deeply loved. Any love that originated with me could change because it was based on emotion, other people, or how I was feeling that day. But God's love is a love that never changes. Constant. Faithful. Unconditional. I could "bank" on a love like that.

One of my favorite speakers, pastor Jason Rollin, frequently says, "People often avoid God, because they don't know what He is full of." Let's look at what the Word says about that:

*The LORD is merciful and compassionate, slow
to get angry and **filled with unfailing love.***
(Psalm 145:8, emphasis added)

What does this verse describe God as being filled with? UNFAILING LOVE. He's not full of anger, hate, or judgement. He is brimming to the top and overflowing with love, mercy, and compassion.

Picture a glass of deep purple grape juice that is filled to the absolute top and has been placed on a couch. And suddenly a little girl skips up in a white dress, and she plops down right next to that cup. What would happen? Mama better find her stain remover; I can tell you that. The sofa and the clothes just got some added color. What if we are the girl, God is the glass, and the couch is the world? If we would only make a move to get closer to Him, what He has would spill over onto us. One touch is all it would take, and that overflowing love He is filled with would become what we're covered in. Because we chose to draw near, the world around us would become saturated with that supernatural love. Being near and reaching out will automatically position us for some added God-color in our hearts and lives. The closer we draw to Him, the more we'll experience what He is filled with: unconditional love.

Pastor Brian Houston explains what encountering God the Father's powerful love will lead to:

> You can enjoy the abundant life filled with the loving presence of your Father and in turn share the unlimited resources of his love with everyone you encounter. With Jesus as our example, we who have been given grace are called to shine it into a dark world. He said, "A new commandment I give to you, that you love one another; as I have loved you, that you also are to love one another. By this, all will

know that you are My disciples, if you have love for one another" (John 13:34-35). Unconditional, inclusive love fuels the big life we long to live.[11]

Now that we know what God is truly full of, we have the choice to decide whether we'll take a step closer to the Father and get a much needed "payday" for our love account, or if we'll continue to strive to love others by relying on ourselves. If we feel empty, drained, and keep asking "am I loving God or others enough?" then there is a good chance our funds are low. Together, let's go to the source of supernatural love and let Him fill us up. Let's get what He's got. We will love God and the people He puts in our path as a result of encountering His great love towards us. To know God is to love Him.

FOOD FOR THE SOUL

I'm a foodie. I enjoy food. I love describing food. I enjoy cooking food. I love eating food. And I love a place that makes some really good food. When I go on vacation, I am not really into sight-seeing, I am more into good-food-eating. Yelp is my favorite app EVER.

As a family with young kids, we don't go out to eat much, but if we do get the opportunity, you can bet we're going to make it count. I have this favorite restaurant. The food is locally sourced and is cooked to culinary perfection, not to mention they have THE BEST coffee around, which is kind of a big deal to me. I mean the coffee makes or breaks the experience in my opinion. Am I right? I know someone is feeling me on that.

After discovering this amazing little farm-to-table restaurant, I've been telling everyone to go check it out. Once you've tasted something so delectable you can't help but sing its praises. No one has told me to recommend this place, but I can't help sharing with all my people where the good food is at. Free advertising!

God's love is like that. A person who has experienced how much God loves them just cannot shut up about it. Once we've had a taste of the real love of God, we are forever changed and start spreading the news. Not only will we share about this incredible love with others, we will demonstrate it as well. Once we've been confronted with the unconditional love the Father has towards us, we love Him and we give of ourselves to others effortlessly because we are filled to the brim with heavenly love. A person who has experienced how much God loves them just cannot keep it a secret. And that is how it is supposed to be.

It is His love which makes the roots of a living tree expand. As a root system develops stronger below the surface, this invisible foundation makes the tree become firm and spread out above ground. The visible result is healthy growth, full foliage, and plentiful fruit. If we're operating in the love of Heaven, people can see. It is a testament to what God's love does. When we live loved we become a free advertisement of His incredible, life-changing, earth-shattering, kingdom-building love.

But maybe you haven't experienced it. Maybe you don't know how much He does loves you. Or maybe you did know it once, but life has left its mark on your heart and you need a fresh encounter to revive your soul.

So, let's ask the question: *How much? How much does God love you?*

Enough to come for you.

True love does not send another to do what only He himself is able to accomplish. So, Jesus came.

> *The LORD looked and was displeased to find there was no justice. He was amazed to see that no one intervened to help the oppressed.* **So he himself stepped in to save them** *with his strong arm, and his justice sustained him.*
>
> (Isaiah 59:15b-16, emphasis added)

God has it made. He lives in the paradise of Heaven and is self-sustaining, so He doesn't need anyone. But He created humanity because it pleased Him. We're the object of His affection and the plan was for us to walk through life with Him, knowing Him and enjoying Him. But after the fall of man, sin tainted the world and all of humanity. We are born with something missing: we are no longer connected to Him from birth. But we want to be. Our hearts long to live knowing the one who made us. Often, we just don't know that is what we're missing. And God wanted our hearts connected to His more than anything. He longed for restored relationship just as we did.

But sin entering the world was no surprise to God. In fact, before He made Earth, he knew what was about to go down, so He planned our redemption in advance and predetermined the solution. He Himself would step in. He would send the ONLY one who could mend the problem, His Son. So when the time was right, Jesus left glory and put on flesh. All of God in human form. Emmanuel, God with us. God the son. And He came.

> *For you know that God paid a ransom to save you from the empty life you inherited from your ancestors. And it was not paid with mere gold or silver, which lose their value. It was the precious blood of Christ, the sinless, spotless Lamb of God. God chose him as your ransom long before the world began...*
>
> (1 Peter 1:18-20a)

He came for us. He came for you. He came because He loves you. He gave up glory to have you back connected with Him.

I once heard someone say, "It wasn't sin that held Jesus to the cross, it was His love for us." God loves everyone who walks this planet. His love isn't earned by our performance but graciously lavished on us because He chooses to do so. His love is based on Himself, not on our record, and He bestows it generously on all. He is love and He gives love; it is His very nature to show love. Our part in all this is to simply receive it as a gift.

Not only does He love all, but God the Father loves you. Individually, uniquely, intimately. Maybe that is hard for you to believe. Maybe you think you haven't earned His love. That He could never love someone like you, not with what you have done. Or perhaps you feel like a "nobody" who isn't worthy. Could it be you don't feel good enough to be loved by anyone?

Let me ask you a question: do you think God the Father loves Jesus? I assume you would believe that.

Well, did you know God loves you as much as He loves Jesus? And I'll prove it. Jesus Himself (while talking to God the Father) said:

> *I am in them and you are in me. May they experience such perfect unity that the world will know that you sent me and that* **you love them as much as you love me.**
>
> (John 17:23, emphasis added)

The first time I read that, I about fell out of my chair. I mean EVERYBODY knows God loves Jesus. Who couldn't? Easy to believe. But, that Jesus himself (who couldn't lie by the way) declares that God loves us just as much. #mindblown.

So, there you have it. That is how much He loves

you. He loves you enough to come and redeem you. He loves you as much as Jesus. You, yes YOU, are loved! VERY MUCH. Soak in that for a bit.

SUPPLY AND DEMAND

In recent years, there has been a big surge in all things superhero. Movies, T-shirts, action figures, toys, plastic weapons, costumes, TV shows... I mean it's everywhere.

My 10-year-old and 4-year-old sons have all the great superhero costumes, and I regularly find my mini-heroes jumping off furniture and slaying imaginary villains.

And it is not just the kids. You better believe my husband and I see every decent DC & Marvel flick that comes out at the theater and we dress up in character. Okay, I'm just playin' about the dress up—or am I?

Our culture is drawn to the supernatural. And I am going to take this opportunity and just say it. Superman is the best. He will always be my favorite. I mean these blog posts about who would win, Hulk vs. Superman, or even better, Batman vs. Superman. PLEASE. Is that a joke? Because I just laughed. Not even a competition. He is the man. Or should I say he is the "super" man? (I just couldn't help myself.)

Superman is all that and a bag of chips, unless... there is Kryptonite around. It is the one element that can drain him of his power and render him weak and practically useless. Even I could take him if Kryptonite were around.

We all have our own personal Kryptonite, don't we? Something or someone that can drain us faster than anything. A few of my current triggers include my children fighting, things not happening in the timeline I had planned for, spending time with negative, half-glass-empty kind of people, and running out of coffee at home (the struggle is real, y'all).

All this "love" talk is inspiring and makes our hearts swell. After I soak in God's love for me, I feel like I can storm the gates of Hell. This supernatural love God has for us and gives to us is powerful, world changing even— but what about when our emotions get the best of us? Or when that relative just made a snide remark? When a news report reveals another horrendous act of evil? A death of a loved one? Or that person just treated us like dirt? In tough situations, it is not so easy to feel loved or show love.

Tragedy, our emotions, other people, and straight up evil are examples of some serious Kryptonite. Love suckers, I like to call them. Even though we've experienced God's love and we start to live knowing we are loved— one thing—one encounter, like traffic, kids fighting, or devastating events can empty our love tank. They can flat out kill our power.

While these things may be our Kryptonite or our power drainers, they have no effect on God. Actually, God cannot be drained. He has an unlimited supply and is the source of supernatural love. We need to rely on Him to fill us with His out-of-this-world love all of the time, but especially when we are facing circumstances such as these and the demands on our life and our love are higher than usual.

So how does that look practically?

First, it is of utmost importance to realize that operating in this supernatural force requires a supernatural guide, specifically, the Holy Spirit. He's our helper and, boy, could we use some help in learning to love, especially when we don't feel like it. Did you know He is the one who disperses God's love in our hearts and makes it accessible to us?

> *And this hope will not lead to disappointment.*
> *For we know how dearly God loves us, because*
> *he has given us the Holy Spirit to fill our hearts*
> *with his love.*
>
> (Romans 5:5)

When the Holy Spirit is guiding your life, His fruit starts showing up. As we are tuned into God's Spirit and following as He leads, our hearts become more and more filled with God's powerful love. Actually, check out what Jesus says the Holy Spirit will do for you:

> *But you will receive **power** when the Holy*
> *Spirit comes upon you. And you will be my*
> *witnesses, telling people about me everywhere*
> *—in Jerusalem, throughout Judea, in Samaria,*
> *and to the ends of the earth.*
>
> (Acts 1:8, emphasis added)

You see that word *power*? It's translated from the Greek word dunamis. That's where we get the English word: DYNAMITE. The Holy Spirit is essential to experience this dynamite-power love, and we need a constant connection with Him if we're going to walk it out and spread it to the ends of the earth.

Secondly, as far as interacting with others goes, it is key to know that God actually loves all people. He doesn't love what all people are doing, but He does love them.

> For **God so loved the world,** *that He gave his*
> *one and only Son, that whoever believes in him*
> *shall not perish but have eternal life.*
> (John 3:16 NIV, emphasis added)

Did you catch "the world?" Yeah, that is everybody. As much as I'd like it to say "the nice people," it doesn't. Because God is good on a whole other level and I wonder if He sees people not as they are, but as they could be if they were restored. He also loves people simply because they are His creation. Knowing that God loves the people who are treating me badly actually plays a role in me being able to be kind to them. I pray, *"God I know you love this person. Would you fill me with your love for them? Please love them through me."* I can't tell you how powerful that prayer and perspective is. It has changed me.

As we ask God to love people through us, we become the vessel He uses to demonstrate His power. Where we are weak He is strong. Again, it's not our love. It is not us striving to love others in our own strength, because with some people that is literally impossible. But, when it is God's heavenly love coming to us, through His Spirit flowing through us, it suddenly becomes possible. In *Wild and Free*, author Jess Connolly shares this truth:

> The same power that comes effortlessly to Him and allows Him to do whatever He wills for the sake of His glory is available to you through the power of the Holy Spirit. Wherever you are, whatever your circumstances—His arm is long, His love is great, and His ways are wild. May you and I become more and more like Him. [12]

When God is doing His supernatural thing through us, we can love anyone He does. For instance, let's say we have a neighbor who has different religious beliefs than us. Now we can either try to argue that our way is the right way, or we can let love do the talking. Bring them a meal when they are sick, bake them cookies, or offer to keep an eye on their house the next time they're going out of town. They say talk is cheap, so don't *talk* about how following Christ is the right way, *show* them how to truly live by loving unconditionally. When a person has a vibrant walk with the Lord, it is evident in how they treat others and people take notice. It is a dynamic way to live and the way that we were always meant to.

The same truth applies to hard situations. The Kryp-tonite of death, sickness, or tragedy can strip our ability to love. In times like that I pray, *"God, I do not feel loved and I do not feel like loving, but I know Your love endures forever. Please continue to fill me with Your supernatural love. Let Your love flow to me and through me, especially when I feel so empty."* And. He. Will. Show. Up.

We know what our Kryptonite is. Maybe it is a sea-sonal issue, maybe it is constant. It might suck the love out of us, but it will never suck the love out of God, because it can't. He is full of love and it endures forever. It knows no end. The mighty love of God is a force like no other and will defeat any natural enemy we face. Run to Him—our source of love—daily to be refilled; His supply is unending.

DIGGING DEEPER

Listen to "To My Knees," by Hillsong Young & Free.

Read Ephesians 5:2.

1. How is your "love account" right now? Do you have love in excess to give away, or are you in need of a deposit of God's love?

2. Think of a person in your life that you are struggling to show love to. What is one thing you can do to practically show them love?

3. Can you recall a moment when you experienced God's love for you in a tangible way? When hard days come that threaten to cause you to doubt His love, remember that moment.

6

LIVING LOVED

Attending a moms group in my early years of mothering was a godsend. It was a morning of relaxation and connection I looked forward to every week. I was able to drop off my kids in a sweet little class where they were taught about Jesus and played with other children their age (yay for babies being socialized), and the moms got to have a breather, drink a cup of coffee, be poured into, and interact with other adults. A win-win for all involved. It was glorious.

One week we were super tight on money, as in our account was at zero. The gas tank in my car was empty, we were out of groceries, and my husband was not getting paid until the following day. All these factors added up to a discouraged mama, who wasn't going to be able to attend my weekly group to be refreshed. I was upset, feeling poor, and eating sautéed corn for a snack because that is all I could find. I am not even joking. Did I mention I was hungry? (Or hangry. However you want to look at it.) And that always makes every circumstance WAY worse than it actually is. *Can I get an Amen?* #justkeepmamafed

My tear-filled eyes were completely focused on my situation, and it looked bleak. Then I was reminded of a familiar Bible verse, "And God shall supply for your needs according to His riches in glory." (Phil 4:19) And I had a choice to make. Would I trust His word and believe He was going to provide, or would I stay fixed on what I could see and wallow in self-pity? I chose to put the spotlight on God and His promise. And in that moment, when my gaze shifted from problem to solution I declared: "God, I trust you. I believe your Word and you are going to meet my need—you always have and you always will." Instantly an unexplainable peace washed over me.

Ten minutes later I got a phone call from my husband, "Hey, you are never going to guess what happened! We just got paid a day early. I'm heading to the bank!" *Come on Jesus!!* That had NEVER happened before. Overcome with thankfulness, I cried tears of joy and relief. God showed me He could be trusted and the importance of keeping my focus on the correct thing that day.

If we're to be known as people who excel at showing love, we need to keep our focus on the right thing. As long as we are solely fixed on our performance and how well we are loving, we are standing on shifting ground. Because there are moments we'll rock it out, but there also are times we'll fall flat on our faces. If our main focus is our love, we'll never be stable or satisfied. But if we look to our

Father's and our Savior's great, overwhelming, unfailing love, our souls can rest securely. We walk out a lifestyle of love by constantly remembering the love God has for us is the *real love* to live by, and now our job is to receive it and reflect it. What we see is what we'll emulate. As we behold His love, we'll show His love. It's ALL about staying fixed on Him and conscious of His affection for us.

> *This is real love—not that we loved God,*
> *but that **he loved us and sent his Son** as a*
> *sacrifice to take away our sins.*
> (1 John 4:10, emphasis added)

Real love, the love to focus on, is God's love for us. That is the Bible. I am not even making this stuff up. It's not about our love, it is about His. His love endures forever. His love saves us. His love changes us. His love empowers us. His love is supernatural.

I love what speaker Christine Caine says about this:

> God's power is not invisible. It's real. It's an undeniable force, and it lives within us. As we fix our eyes on him, we see his love, we taste his power, and it feeds us. It helps us grow stronger... [13]

You know, some really cool things happened in the Bible when people focused on and declared God's faithful love. One of my favorites is the time a massive army was marching against God's people. You can find the whole story in 2 Chronicles 20.

> *After consulting the people, the king appointed singers to walk ahead of the army, singing to the Lord and praising him for his holy splendor. This is what they sang: "Give thanks to the Lord; his faithful love endures forever!" At the very moment they began to sing and give praise, the Lord caused the armies of Ammon, Moab, and Mount Seir to start fighting among themselves... Not a single one of the enemy had escaped.*
>
> (2 Chronicles 20:21, 22 & 24b)

If you think about it, this story is kind of crazy, right? This army is going to war and they put the artsy, in-touch-with-their-emotions worship team on the front line instead of the skilled, mean, lean killing machine warriors? To others, that seems a little odd and just plain wrong, but sometimes with God you have to be willing to do the abnormal to see the supernatural.

So, the praise team went ahead of the army and as they sang about God's amazing, faithful, enduring love, the enemy army turned on themselves and destroyed each other. God's people didn't have to do anything... except focus on and declare God's love. Crazy, but effective.

Maybe singing songs that proclaim the unfailing

love of God is actually warfare. When we are facing our enemies, perhaps all we need to do to see victory is trust in and reaffirm God's love for us. Yes, acknowledge the battle: we lose our job, we had a death in the family, we are facing sickness, we are anxious, depression is setting in... very real threats are happening all around us, but even so... God's faithful love is there. We can choose to say, "Yes I am going through this struggle, but I know still God loves me and His love never ends." Knowing we are loved empowers us to push through and overcome.

A person who knows they are loved by God is unstoppable. Real love is God's love for us. Real love needs to be our focus. Real love is the most powerful force on the planet.

STAY A LITTLE WHILE

"When can we meet for coffee?" I was stoked as I read the text message and couldn't wait to respond, "ASAP!" I enjoy being around and connecting with a lot of people at church, small group, or a party, but I also cherish those precious conversations had over a warm cup of coffee. It is then, in those intimate settings, where you dig in and really open up about life. Conversations like this don't usually take place during big parties where you need to make sure you say "Hi!" to everyone, these are the coffee-dates you intentionally set aside time for deeper connection.

I love that feeling I have when I walk away after

having coffee with a dear friend. Do you know what I am talking about? It's like your bucket is full, your heart is happy, and suddenly life just got a little bit brighter. We were designed for community. We're meant to commune with God and others. When you think about a tree's roots, it isn't just the soil itself which is important for healthy growth. Roots need the right nutrients to be present for optimal growth, and we too need nourishment from others to reach our fullest potential. In order for us to grow in greater relationship with God the Father, Son, and Spirit, we will need supportive relationships in our lives which will nurture us to grow in love and inspire us to go deeper with God.

Do you have relationships that are encouraging in nature? A good measure is to ask yourself, "Do I come away from our meeting feeling positive and encouraged, or negative and pessimistic?" There are some people who have this inviting presence, making others want to linger a bit longer and spend more time in their company. I love when I have a life-giving encounter with a friend or a loved one that leaves me feeling refreshed. Just as healthy relationships are designed to bring us life, God also wants us continually connected with Him. His desire is for us to remain in His love and be revived by His presence in our lives—daily.

I have loved you even as the Father has loved me. **Remain in my love.**
(John 15:9, emphasis added)

Now that we've heard about how much God is in love with us and how powerful the encounter of that love can be, we cannot go back to life as usual. We must remain in that love, forever knowing we are the beloved of God. Nothing will change that. Yes, we go on to grow in other areas, but it is essential to our growth to possess a constant awareness of Christ's love for us. This must be a foundational truth we constantly cling to. We must remain ever conscious of the lavish, life-altering love of God our Savior.

Banning Liebscher, Senior pastor of Jesus Culture Sacramento, is one of my favorite authors. He has an incredible revelation of the love of God; check out what he shares about abiding in Christ's love:

> The new breed of revivalist that is emerging in the earth is learning the secret of abiding in the love of Jesus, and thus they are burning with passion for Him. Their hearts are molten—liquefied by His unquenchable love—and they are being poured out upon others. They will be known as Burning Ones, whose lives ignite revival fires across the globe. Because they walk in the revelation of friendship with God, they do not work *for* Him but *with* Him. They are *lovers* of God, not *employees* of God. The lives of lovers stand out because they are not motivated by fame or fortune but by a deep love for Jesus. [14]

You see, once we're grounded and remaining in the love that God has for us, our hearts are set on fire with His explosive power. It is then we overflow with His passion and begin impacting the world around us.

My command is this: Love each other as I have loved you.
(John 15:12, NIV)

Jesus said, "Love others, as I have loved you." His command is preceded by an experience. Meaning, we must know His love in order to show His love. Jesus isn't pushy, so He isn't speaking with a demanding tone and shouting, "You better love people!" It's more like, "Hey guys, once you realize how much I love you, you are going to love others SO well." And if we find ourselves not loving well, maybe we need a fresh encounter and reminder. We must begin with the deposit if we want to end in success. If we want to change the world, a good place to start is by connecting with the one who made it. The personal experience comes first and the walking it out comes second. Trying to love without the means results in a discouraged life of failure. But finding ourselves drenched in the love of God Almighty results in a life of dynamite power.

So I am going to say it again, because it is important and one cannot hear this enough. God loves you. He takes great pleasure in you. You are valuable to Him. He created you beautifully and He does not make mistakes. He is good and He is love and He wants to reveal Himself to you in that way. I hope you will let him, because you are His beloved.

> *Dear friends, let us continue to love one another, for love comes from God. Anyone who loves is a child of God and knows God. But anyone who does not love does not know God, for God is love.*
> (1 John 4:7-8)

Something is just different about a person who is in love. They light up the whole room. Well, when we REAL-LY know God, not in a book-knowledge way, but in an experiential way, we fall in love with Him. And when we are in love with our Creator, we don't just light up the room, we become the light of the world because our love is backed by kingdom power. Our intimate relationship with Him fuels us to care for people in a whole new way. As we show this compelling love to the world, we are truly acting like our Father, because that is who He is and what He does. God is love.

Life will happen. Good things and bad things will come our way. But through it all, we must continue to stay connected to the love that God has for us personally, this is what keeps us strong. We have to pursue a continual filling and experiencing of God's amazing love to be able to walk out His mandate to love. He designed us to need to be connected to Him in order to live life to the fullest.

But I am like an olive tree, thriving in the house
of God. I will always trust in God's unfailing
love.

(Psalm 52:8)

I want to be like this strong tree, don't you? When our roots are sunk deep into the love that God has for us, we flourish. We need a generation of people who are thriving in the presence of God and locked into his power if we are going to change the world. We will live abundantly and love powerfully as we are joined to God and abiding in His unfailing, never-ending love. Bank on it. Walk with it. Stay in it.

FAN INTO FLAME

Loving intensely: it is doable, with God's help. What I have learned is when His love invades our hearts, it changes us, and in turn we change our world. The supernatural, ultra-powerful, and explosive love of God is earth shattering... in a good way.

If we're going to see this dynamite love happen in our lives and communities, we have to remember: loving starts with God. As we're connecting with His Spirit and He fills our hearts with divine love, we step into the supernatural realm and begin loving like He does. Once God is the source, and we understand we're the vessel He pours His power into, we love with the strength and grace He provides. He starts loving people through us and we get to watch. It's powerful.

As we walk through life understanding we're deeply loved by God (as is everyone else), our perspective changes. When we pray, God gives us His heart for people and we start seeing others in a whole new light. Then we can love others who act, talk, and believe differently than us.

We can't produce lasting fruit, like love, on our own. So, when Jesus says we're to love our enemies, it seems like a crazy statement, but it is only crazy if we try to do it without His help. And if we're honest, people aren't really our enemy. There is one enemy of us all: Satan. He will try to get you to hate the people who God loves. But if we pray that God opens our heart to all people and allow Him to use us, we will witness miraculous things. If a tree has solid roots, strengthened with God the Father's unconditional love, it naturally produces fruit to bless others with.

Let's take a look at one final passage. It is, in my opinion, the greatest chapter in the Bible on love. Paul starts out by saying if we have all the gifts of the Spirit, but don't possess the supernatural love of God, all our serving and ministering is pointless. How often do we make developing our gifts our focus and skip over love? God's word says love is the highest goal (1 Corinthians 14:1) and should be top priority.

Now, I'm going to do something a little unconventional with 1 Corinthians 13. Since God *is* love, I am going to replace the word love with God and see if we can grasp what it would look like to walk in love.

God is patient.

God is kind.

God does not envy.

God does not boast.

God is not proud.

God does not dishonor others.

God is not self-seeking.

God is not easily angered.

God keeps no record of wrongs. (My personal favorite.)

God does not delight in evil.

God rejoices with the truth.

God always protects.

God always trusts.

God always hopes.

God always perseveres.

God never fails.

(Adapted from 1 Corinthians 13:4-8, NIV)

If that is how God operates, and we are His children, shouldn't we live that way, too? With His help, we can and we will. When we live loved, we ignite something powerful in our land. We were born for such a time as this and we are called to do great things!

*So, this is my prayer: that your love will flourish
and that **you will not only love much but well**.*
(Philippians 1:9, MSG, emphasis added)

I pray above all else that we fall in love with the One who is head over heels in love with us. I pray we allow the Holy Spirit's wind to fan into flame the love of Christ until it is a roaring wildfire consuming all that we are and all that we do. I pray our life is set ablaze, full of God's divine passion, and that we walk in the explosive power to shift families, churches, cities, kingdoms, countries, and the whole earth. It is time to go. Let's light up our world with Holy fire by showing them The Awesome One's dynamite love!

HE IS MY HEAVENLY FATHER
I AM A LOVED CHILD OF GOD

DIGGING DEEPER

Listen to "Wake," by Hillsong Young & Free.

Read John 13:35.

1. How can you practice "remaining" in God's love? List one thing you can do daily to help you focus on His love for you.

2. Can you think of a time where you were going through a hard situation, but the love of God helped you through it?

3. Is there anyone or anything that you are feeling especially called to love right now? What groups, organizations, places, or people are you uniquely positioned to deeply love and invest in?

EVEN THE SMALLEST FLICKER OF LIGHT POSSESSES THE POWER TO ILLUMINATE THE DARKEST PLACE. WE ARE THE LIGHT OF THE WORLD, BECAUSE WE HAVE THE LIGHT OF LIFE. BUT WHAT EXACTLY MAKES US RADIANT? OUR SAVIOR, AND THE TRUTH ABOUT OUR IDENTITY IN HIM. IF WE ARE TO LIGHT UP THIS WORLD AND SHATTER ALL THE DARKNESS, WE HAVE TO KNOW GOD THE SON.

SHATTERING
LIGHT

THE LIGHT SHINES IN THE DARKNESS, AND THE DARKNESS CAN NEVER EXTINGUISH IT.

JOHN 1:5

7

I KNOW THAT'S TRUE

One year, I received the sweetest Mother's Day gift from my little 4-year-old, Jack. At preschool he planted a seed in a little pot painted with his fingerprints, watered it lovingly for weeks, and by Mother's Day, it had produced a beautiful flower. I placed this sweet little bloom on the counter behind the sink where I do dishes — somewhere I would see it a lot (and thus be reminded to water it) so it wouldn't join the graveyard of neglected plants I've managed to kill over the last few years! Within a day the blossom was no longer facing the sink or me but had completely turned toward the nearest window. A plant, if positioned in the shade, will stretch its branches to ensure it gets as much sunlight as possible and grows to its fullest potential.

We've learned the magnitude of being rooted in the love of Father God, and now we're going to talk about how life-changing it is for us to be positioned in the light of knowing God the Son: Jesus. What a name — the name above every other. He is God our Savior and the Good Shepherd who will leave ninety-nine sheep who are "found" and go out to search for the one which is lost (even though other shepherds may think this wandering sheep is insignificant—but not our God).

I know about looking for lost things. I used to lose stuff. ALL. THE. TIME. Items such as my phone, my license, and my wallet (you know, all the necessities for driving and functioning responsibly) have all been MIA more than once in my home. I remember one time losing my favorite pair of jeans. I looked everywhere for them. My outfit would not have been complete without these particular pants. I emptied all my drawers, went through the dirty clothes, and checked the wash, only to come up empty handed. After a long, exhausting search (but for real, it was probably only 20 minutes—however in the moment, it felt like an eternity), I finally threw in the towel and gave up. It was then that I looked down and found my jeans. I was wearing them y'all. For the love. #truestory

Have you ever looked for something so diligently and not given up until it was found? (Keys, anyone?) Well, Jesus tells us to look into a couple of things before we run after anything else, and we find this in Matthew 6:33:

> *But seek first his kingdom and his righteousness,*
> *and all these things will be given to you as well.*
> (Matthew 6:33, NIV)

When we are familiar with a scripture and have heard it many times it is easy to read it quickly and think, "Yeah, I know what that is saying." And for a long time I read this verse and believed the basic point was that we need to put God first. Now, putting God first is absolutely a good thing, but this scripture isn't saying that exactly. What two things are we are told to diligently look for and seek out first and foremost? Read it again. Go ahead, I'll wait. Then meet me back here.

What is Jesus telling us to specifically look for?

God's Kingdom and His righteousness.

Discovering the meaning behind these two truths are essential to knowing God as Savior, that's why we are told to seek them first, before all else. If understanding more about His kingdom and His righteousness results in ALL THINGS being given to us as well, I'd say they are worth a good portion of our attention.

Remember scavenger hunts? I loved going on them as a child, so naturally, I love putting them on. We often give our children at least one larger gift at Christmas and send them off with lots of clues leading them to their surprise at the end of the adventure. Well, similarly, God has hidden the meaning of this verse in the Bible and He wants us to unearth these valuables. It is our great privilege to go on this spiritual treasure hunt.

It is God's privilege to conceal things and the king's privilege to discover them. (Proverbs 25:2)

Since I believe half of the fun is in the personal discovery, we're only going to touch on His kingdom (because this topic is a whole book in itself). I encourage you to take time and dig a little deeper into the subject. To get your wheels spinning, I'll mention that the Kingdom of God is the place where God has full reign. So of course, Heaven is a place His will and His authority are fully recognized, operated in, and complete. But, if we recall the Lord's prayer, Jesus prayed, "Your Kingdom come, your will be done ON EARTH as it is in Heaven." Jesus taught us to ask for God's kingdom to come down to earth. I think as believers, we should absolutely look forward to the freedom we'll experience in Heaven but not give up on this world in our journey to get there. God actually wants believers to pray with His Son for the power and attributes of Heaven to invade earth through us. (If you are intrigued to search this out a bit further, here is a tip to get you started: look up every reference to His Kingdom, God's kingdom or the Kingdom of Heaven in the New Testament and read them side by side. Connect those dots. Happy hunting!)

But, His righteousness *is* something we're going to explore together because it is one of my favorite things to talk about. Spoiler alert: I'm about to go public with this thing because the treasure of understanding His righteousness is life-changing. Now, I know at first glance this topic might sound a little boring, but I'm here to tell you it's not. It has changed EVERYTHING for me. I'm talking Every. Thing. Merely scratching the surface on His righteousness exploded new growth in my walk, and it literally transformed me from a shy Christian who was afraid to share my faith to a bold person who finally has some good news to share. It brought me from death to life, shattered the darkness and propelled me into light, and now I want everyone to experience this power. So, I intend to blow the roof off this thing.

I want to start by asking a question: What is the gospel about? It's ok to be unsure, because we're going to read what the Bible has to say about it. Take a look at this passage of scripture:

> *For I am not ashamed of the gospel, because it is the power of God that brings salvation to everyone who believes: first to the Jew, then to the Gentile. **For in the gospel the righteousness of God is revealed—a righteousness that is by faith** from first to last, just as it is written: "The righteous will live by faith."*
>
> (Romans 1:16-17, NIV, emphasis added)

This verse highlights several important things, but for our study we're going to hone in on what the gospel unveils. According to the scripture above, what does the gospel actually reveal?

The righteousness of God which comes by faith. Anyone thinking, *Okay that is great, now what does it mean?* We're about to find out.

I have to mention how Paul (the writer of this Bible passage) makes it clear that God's righteousness—which is the very thing Jesus told us to search for—is achieved by faith or believing, not action or accolades. Tuck this little factoid away in your pocket and we'll pull it out later. Understanding this integral part of the gospel is powerful, and with this in mind, our plan is to dig a little deeper into the meaning of God's righteousness. But before we do, how about we pause and whisper a prayer to invite Jesus to light our way—because we are going to need His guidance.

SELF VS. SAVIOR

I think I'm really a Greek trapped in an American's body. Okay, all jokes aside, I am absolutely fascinated by the history, architecture, and beautiful country of Greece (I've not been there, but I live vicariously through people's Instagram images of their Greek vacations—I'll get there one day). And don't even get me started on the food and drink. Strong coffee, Greek salad with salty feta cheese, and baklava dripping in honey. *Mmmmmm*. My mouth was literally watering as I typed that.

This interest is not just found in the food and culture, but at the risk of sounding nerdy, I have to tell you I love the Greek language. Greek is so much more descriptive than English. Where we have one word, such as "love," they have six words (philia, ludus, storge, eros, pragma, agape) we would translate to the same English word. Their descriptions would say love like a friend, playful love, love for a child, intimate love, longstanding love, or love for God and man. We just say love, but there are different kinds of love; the Greek language leaves no room for confusion.

The New Testament was initially written in Greek. I know everyone has their favorite Bible translation, but the only completely accurate one is the original one. In the last section, we learned God's righteousness is revealed in the gospel. In order for us to comprehend what "His righteousness" *really* means, we have to see how it is defined in the Greek language and then piece our new-found information together with other scriptures. We'll let the Bible interpret the Bible, y'all.

When you see the word "righteousness" in the New Testament, it is usually translated from the Greek word: dikaiosuné (pronounced dik-ah-yos-oo'-nay). I'll try not to get too geeky on you, but knowing the Greek meaning is going to prove vital to our understanding of God's righteousness, so bear with me for second—I promise it will be worth it.

dikaiosuné: *righteousness of which God is the source or author, but practically: a divine righteousness. The condition acceptable to God.*[15]

Now, knowing the definition, let's put Matthew 6:33 into a new light. Jesus is telling us to discover God's divine righteousness, which is the only way to be right with God.

So, if we read Jesus's words in Matthew chapter six, then take a little hop, skip, and a leap over to Romans, we'll begin to put the pieces together of what His righteousness means for us and how exactly we *are* "made right with God." Before we read the scripture, think of all the religions in the world and even the way things used to be under the law in the Old Testament. Consider the lists of rules which must be obeyed in order to be accepted, known as devout, or have an ideal afterlife. Now we're about to see how (through Jesus), Christianity is set apart from every other religion.

> *God did this to demonstrate his righteousness, for he himself is fair and just, and he makes sinners right in his sight when they believe in Jesus. Can we boast, then, that we have done anything to be accepted by God? No, because our acquittal is not based on obeying the law. It is based on faith.* **So we are made right with God through faith and not by obeying the law.**
> (Romans 3:26b- 28, emphasis added)

Mmmmmmm AMEN! First, we learned that hidden in the gospel, God unveiled the path to His righteousness. Remember the factoid we tucked away about becoming righteous and how it is only achieved by faith? It's time to pull that out because now, we see what His righteousness actually is. It is referring to God's way of being righteous, and the only way people can be right with Him—shockingly—has nothing to do with behavior and everything to do with belief. *What?!?* Yeah, I said that. But don't take my word for it, the verse I just shared says it is not our obedience, but our faith in Jesus which makes us right with God. We cannot *do* anything to be right, we're only righteous by faith. Period.

Look back at the passage we just read. It teaches us when we believe in Jesus, God makes the sinner (notice the verse doesn't say the good person or the obedient, it says the one who has sinned: the one who has messed up) right in His sight. His divine righteousness is given to those who believe in Jesus, not to those who necessarily have their act together, but to them whose faith is in Christ alone. *Can I get a hallelujah?!*

If you are skeptical of believing this, recall all the men and women listed in the Hebrews Chapter 11 "Hall of Faith," as many Christians call it. The people in this passage are not remembered for their mistakes—which include getting drunk, lying, cheating, murder, prostitution, and adultery to name a few. Obviously, these biblical heroes didn't have a perfect track record. So why did they make the list?

Their faith.

It's called the Hall of Faith, not the Hall of Obedience or the Hall of Mistakes. *I know that's true!* Faith is what is important and it is what pleases God. (It is IMPOSSIBLE to please God without faith..." Hebrews 11:6, NIV says.) And please hear my heart, I'm not saying obedience isn't important; we should absolutely obey God's leading and His Word. But as believers, we don't obey to get justified, we obey because we *are* justified by having faith in our Savior. We are obedient because this is what justified, right-with-God, righteous people do. We want to. We are compelled to. It's who we are.

Our self-righteousness, obedience, and striving never work to make ourselves right with a holy God. However, Jesus's righteousness does work and He has given His followers: **His righteousness.** Everyone needs Jesus to be right with God. This is why He is the only way to the Father.

This is how Christianity is different. Where other religions say we must *do* to get to God, the Bible says our God came down and *did* for us what we could not achieve on our own. God was like, *wow, these guys are never going to live up to my standard of holiness. I can see I will have to fix this myself.* So He did.

When Jesus exchanged positions with us and took our place on the cross, He gifted us His righteous standing so all we need to do is stop trying to work our way into God's good graces and realize because of Jesus we are already there! Now that is an awesome Savior right there. *Come on somebody?!*

Speaker Tricia Gunn shares about the results of getting rid of self-righteousness in her book, *Unveiling Jesus*:

> If we remove all attempts to make ourselves righteous before God and trust that we are righteous through Christ, then our conscience would be free

from guilt and unworthiness. If we believed we are worthy, we would have no hesitation receiving anything from God. Getting rid of self-righteousness is the key to living a miraculous faith-filled life![16]

So how exactly do we step away from a self-righteous mindset? Let's take a closer look at what God the Son achieved at Calvary. At the cross, Jesus didn't deserve our sin to be placed on Him, but He took it and paid for it. We didn't deserve His righteousness to be placed on us but, by faith, it's a gift we're given to wear. When we understand we wear what He earned because He wore what we earned, then we can leave our self-righteousness behind. We traded places at the cross. His righteous position became our position the moment we trusted in Jesus as our Savior, our Messiah, our Sacrifice. Starting at our decision and extending through all of eternity, we are hidden "In Christ." This is the divine exchange and it is totally AWESOME.

I love how Isaiah explains what happens at Salvation:

I am overwhelmed with joy in the Lord my God! **For he has dressed me with the clothing of salvation and draped me in a robe of righteousness.** *I am like a bridegroom dressed for his wedding or a bride with her jewels.*

(Isaiah 61:10, emphasis added)

If you believe in Jesus, you are the bride of Christ. He cleaned you, paid for all of your sins (even the ones you haven't done yet), and wrapped you up in His own righteousness. Glorious. This robe He dressed you in isn't coming off. What God has done no one can undo: not you, not the devil, and not even sin.

> *From eternity to eternity I am God. No one can snatch anyone out of my hand.* **No one can undo what I have done.**
>
> (Isaiah 43:13, emphasis added)

As a believer, you have an eternal security. Eternal life does not start after you die. It starts now. This is how Jesus himself describes eternal life:

> **Now this is eternal life: that they know you, the one true God, and Jesus Christ,** *whom you have sent.*
>
> (John 17:3, NIV, emphasis added)

Eternal life *is* knowing God and the Messiah He sent: Jesus. This verse makes it crystal clear that unending life begins with intimately knowing God the Father and His son, Jesus. As we unearth what our Savior accomplished through His sacrifice and resurrection, we truly come alive and get to do this life and all of eternity with God. Just like a tree needs constant exposure to the sun to create unending energy in order to thrive, knowing Jesus and what He did for us supplies us "living trees" with constant vitality. Jesus opened the door for us to know the God of the universe personally by giving us His righteousness, so we could enter His presence and commune with Him any time. This is a huge part of the gospel!

There are two kinds of righteousness: our own and His. Our self-righteousness is our own natural attempt to do right—to be acceptable before God. His righteousness is the divine way to be accepted before God, earned and sustained by Jesus, and given to us supernaturally by believing in the finished work of Christ. This is what it all comes down to: Will we trust in our effort or in Jesus's accomplishment?

BELIEVE IT OR NOT

We are movie people. Every weekend, we have a family movie night. Through all of our moves, this is one tradition which has stood the test of relocation. We love going to the movies, streaming them on Netflix, or renting them on iTunes—it's a favorite pastime in our home. The buttery popcorn, the cuddles on the couch, the thrill of a great story, and the disconnect from our phones, all add up to a GREAT night!

Have you ever had someone tell you a movie was really good, only to discover after watching the flick that you and your friend apparently have different definitions of what makes a "good movie?" Been there. And it was a complete waste of two hours! Now when I begin watching a recommended movie, I kind of have my guard up. I keep wondering if it will take a turn for the worse or have a bad ending and ruin our whole movie night experience. When I hear a movie is good, I nod my head and respond, "Oh, Okay," but silently I am thinking: *Well, I'll be the judge of that*. Does that make me a movie snob? Probably, but when I hear good I expect to see "Lord-of-the-Rings-caliber" GOOD. *Can I get an AMEN?!*

I tell you this because I am about to share something good with you. And this is legit good. It's not a movie recommendation (although I have a few of those if you need one). This is something WAY better. This is REAL good news—actually THE BEST news. With all the bad reports we hear in the media, it is about time something good is shared. It is easy to see all of the negative in the world, in others, and in ourselves. I say GOOD deserves a chance in the spotlight. We're going to look back at the chapter in Romans that talks about the gospel in another version.

> *For I am not ashamed of this **Good News about Christ**. It is the power of God at work, saving everyone who believes—the Jew first and also the Gentile. **This Good News tells us how God makes us right in his sight. This is accomplished from start to finish by faith.** As the Scriptures say, "It is through faith that a righteous person has life."*
>
> (Rom 1:16-17, emphasis added)

This is the best news I've ever heard! The "good news" is that God makes His children right in His sight—we talked through this point previously. It is what happens when we trust in Jesus as our Savior. This is the gospel. Now, here is where the news gets *really* good: this is a once-and-for-ever deal. When we step into a relationship with the Lord, He makes us right with Himself, and throughout our entire walk with God (notice how the verse points out from start to finish), He is the one who makes us right in His sight. Every Christian whose faith is in Christ is right before God, standing in a righteous position. Now, this doesn't mean every decision we make, every word we say, or every action we take is always right, but our position is—and always will be—righteous.

I haven't always known that.

I used to think my relationship with God was based on my behavior. I thought the "gospel" meant having faith in Jesus as the Son of God, for a fresh start and to secure my entrance into Heaven, but I did not believe Jesus kept me right with God, especially if I messed up. I was ultra-focused on my performance and had little faith in Christ's. But now, I realize my relationship with God is based on Jesus and my faith in Him. Let's look back at Romans 1:17. Who makes us right with God? Us or God? How is this done? Our performance? Or Faith in His performance?

This Good News tells us how God makes us right in his sight. This is accomplished from start to finish by faith.

God does it. We have to give Him the credit. God makes us right with Himself. Faith in Jesus and His work accomplishes it. We are in a position of being right with God because He made us so. All we have to do is believe. Our part is faith. We must have faith that God makes us right; it's not us, not our performance, and not our adherence to religious traditions. I'll illustrate it in another way. I have three kids, and just because they don't always obey the way I think an Olafsson should obey, it doesn't mean they stop being my child (or an Olafsson). Being righteous, like being a child of God, is not an obedience thing, but a positional thing.

Pastor Judah Smith really brings this point home in one of his sermons:

> Jesus took our penalty, so we could take His blessing. Jesus took our judgement, so we could receive His righteousness. Jesus took our place... If you simply believe in Jesus and receive His once and for all sacrifice, your standing with God in this world according to the Father is identical with Jesus. You are fully and completely and entirely and eternally right with God. And, you cannot be un-right. When you are right with God it is permanent and it is eternal. Oh, we got something to sing about, we got something to talk about, we got something to

rejoice about, and clap about. The fact is Jesus took our place—we take His place. There was a switch, by simply believing and now I am right with God forever and ever without end.[17]

Hallelujah! This being right with God forever situation is REAL good news for all of us who screw up on a regular basis.

Believing I am right with God is easier on some days than others. Like when I've had my quiet time, led my Bible study, or prayed for my friends. On those days, I am feeling pretty good about our relationship. But when I've yelled one too many times, been so busy I haven't talked to God all day, or honked at crazy drivers in traffic, on those days I'm feeling like I'm on the "outs." How could I be right with Him, when I didn't exactly obey the commandment to love today?! Well let's see what the word says about the correlation between obedience and being right with God.

*For no one can ever be made right with God by doing what the law commands. The law simply shows us how sinful we are. But now **God has shown us a way to be made right with him without keeping the requirements of the law,** as was promised in the writings of Moses and the prophets long ago. **We are made right with God by placing our faith in Jesus Christ. And this is true for everyone who believes,** no mat-*

ter who we are. For everyone has sinned; we all fall short of God's glorious standard. **Yet God, with undeserved kindness, declares that we are righteous.** *He did this through Christ Jesus when he freed us from the penalty for our sins.*
(Romans 3:20-24, emphasis added)

I don't know about other people, but EVERY time I read that first sentence I think, *WHAT did that just say? Like, for real, did I read it right?* As a matter of fact, the first time I read this passage to another Christian they asked me what book I was reading from, and they were shocked when I told them I was actually quoting the Bible! I am telling you it is mind blowing. You can't "do" to be right with God?! This sounds scandalous! Such is grace. So, if you need to do a double take of that passage, I COMPLETELY understand, go ahead, I'll meet you back here.

Brace yourselves, I'm about to say something: The law, the 10 Commandments, are not rules we must follow to stay in fellowship with God. Don't take my word for it, that is what the Bible says. Shocking! The law is actually an impossible standard which exposes our faults. It shows us that we sin, that we're not perfect, and that we all fall short of God's standard. The law puts us all on a level playing field. No one is perfect (no matter how amazing their Instagram feed is—I'm just sayin'). Not one person. Except Jesus. And either you are perfect, or you need a Savior. Meaning: We all need Jesus.

I've heard people try to argue that "the law" Paul was referring to in this scripture was the extra laws listed in Leviticus and additional regulations the Pharisees had imposed on the Jews—not the 10 Commandments. But in another letter Paul mentions the law which was associated with the "old way" again, and he explains which law he meant.

> *The old way, with laws etched in stone, led to death...*
>
> (2 Corinthians 3:7a)

Just so we're all on the same page, which laws were written on stone? The 10 Commandments. This set of laws points out our sins, and striving to follow them to ensure our fellowship with God leads to death because we can't do it. Some of them, yes, but not all. And Jesus even took it a step further when He preached the sermon on the mount by basically saying, "If you even think about breaking these rules, you're guilty of committing them." (See Matthew 5:28) We simply cannot keep these laws consistently. The previous way laid out in the Old Covenant was an agreement of obedience to attain right standing before God. But this covenant actually breeds death because the Commandments cannot be kept and are meant to expose our inadequacy and our need for a Savior.

The law, written on stone, and the extra unbearable, unachievable Levitical laws all point to Someone. To a person who could keep them, the one who was truly righteous: Jesus Christ. Let's jump back to the Romans passage to learn more about the way God has shown us how to be made right with Him. We'll pick up in Romans chapter three, verse 21.

Now God has shown us a way to be made right with him without keeping the law... by placing our faith in Jesus.

Are we made right with God by obeying the law, by how we act, or by our faith in Jesus? What does the Bible say?

Faith in Jesus. *Hallelujah!*

And good gracious it keeps going! How many of us know Romans 3:23? We all sin. If we've been a Christian for any amount of time we probably are VERY familiar with this. We ALL fall short. Oh, believers know Romans 3:23, but how many of us could spout off Romans 3:24? It says:

Yet God, with undeserved kindness, declares that we are righteous. He did this through Christ Jesus when he freed us from the penalty for our sins.

Yet God.

This is like the biggest "Yet God" in the Bible! God himself declares we are righteous. The Greek word for righteous here is:

dikaioó(dik-ah-yo'-o) and it means: *The believer is "made righteous/justified" (/dikaióō) by the Lord, cleared of all charges (punishment) related to their sins.*[18]

Dikaioó is often translated justified, but I never really knew what justified meant. *Anyone else feel this way?* But now, I know it means "made right with God." Jesus is righteous, and now His followers are too because we are "In Christ." Christians seem to be very comfortable with calling ourselves sinners. But what does God call us? What does He declare us to be?

Righteous. Justified. Right in His sight. *Come on now, that's good news!*

How could we be? He made us righteous through the sacrifice of Jesus. God did the whole thing and our part is believing and receiving what He did. This is when unparalleled spiritual growth happens. Just like a tree standing in full sun grows higher, stronger, and fuller, so we too flourish as we stand in the full light of the Son.

> *The righteous will flourish like a palm tree, they*
> *will grow like a cedar of Lebanon;*
> (Psalm 92:12, NIV)

We are the righteous. I mean, this revelation alone opens up a whole slew of scriptures I never thought applied to me because I believed I wasn't good enough to earn the title. But as it turns out, Jesus was good enough, and He gave righteousness to me and all who choose to believe in Him. What an undeserved gift of grace!

In *Destined To Reign*, pastor Joseph Prince shares about this gift.

> Grace does not point to your efforts, your performance or your doing. It makes nothing of man's self-efforts and points completely to Jesus's efforts and what He has done. The law makes one self-conscious. It is always asking, "What must I do?" But grace makes one Christ-conscious. It is always asking, "What has Jesus done?" Under law, the burden is on you to perform. Under grace, the burden is on what Christ has performed on the cross… Jesus came to reveal grace, and the yoke of grace is easy and light because it involves none of you and all of Christ. He has borne the burden of sin on your behalf. Under grace, your part is to only believe on Jesus Christ, and when you believe you are blessed and made righteous! [19]

Should a shift take place? Should we change the way we identify ourselves to the way God identifies and sees us? Should we call ourselves what God does, and come into agreement with His words? God declares we are righteous. So we must be, because He never lies. If we want to see breakthrough in an area of sin, should we continually call ourselves sinners, or should our words align with Heaven's declarations and call ourselves righteous? I think it's time we look at ourselves from a Heavenly perspective, through the lens of the "good news," and recognize the amazing thing Jesus did for us. That's our awesome God.

DIGGING DEEPER

Listen to "I Will Boast In Christ," by Hillsong Worship.

Read Galatians 2:16.

1. Is it easier for you to call yourself a sinner or to call yourself righteous? Why?

2. How do you think your view of yourself as a child of God would change if you called yourself righteous, as God does?

3. How do you think your view of God the Father would change if you fully believed you were righteous, as He calls you?

8

ACT THE PART

Once, I was a victim of identity theft. Oh yeah, someone tried to get away with impersonating me. And this person was the old Amber. This was not a normal stolen identity case, it was spiritual. Something very discouraging happened: I ran into my own "Kryptonite." At first, I responded negatively. (As in, I vented to my husband about my hurts, and let's just say, I was not speaking very life-giving words.) Thank goodness he is a safe and stable person, and he reeled me back in and reminded me to love and show grace. We all need people in our life who we can open up to and will gently remind us of our true mission here on earth.

The truth is, this one outburst left me feeling condemned, and it got worse before it got better. Ever notice how condemnation always breeds more and more pessimism? It's like I forgot who I was. I was moping around and turned from being a life-giving fountain to a life-sucking drain. In this fog, I felt similar to a sheep who had wandered off from stable ground. There are times in life this happens, so how do we combat this confusion and discouragement?

We must take our struggle to our Shepherd.

So, I got alone with Jesus, we talked, and He reminded me of two things:

- There is NO CONDEMNATION for those who are In Christ. (Romans 8:1) And while yes, I had missed the mark, God was not condemning me for it.
- He spoke a sentence I will NEVER forget "Daughter, you are righteous, now act that way."

Like a key which opened the lock of my chains keeping me tied to guilt and reckless behavior, those two simple truths set me free to be who I *really* was. What we call ourselves becomes our identity. Our words turn into a self-fulfilling prophecy, meaning: we will become what we say we are. If we call ourselves sinners, this can influence the way we act. On the other hand, if we call ourselves righteous, we begin to act accordingly. Our actions will line up with what we believe about ourselves.

I've noticed sometimes Christians can throw around "churchy" words and assume everyone knows their meaning. I think our "Identity in Christ" is one such phrase. To put it simply, as believers we are now found in Christ. When God looks at us, He does not see us apart from Jesus, He sees us clothed in Christ. Our identity is not based on what we do or have done, our identity is found in who we belong to. For instance, take my children. Just because they don't have perfect conduct does not mean they aren't in my family anymore. They were born into our family, they remain in our family, and their behavior doesn't change this. Similarly, as Christ-followers we will ALWAYS be found "in Christ" regardless of our actions. If behavior did not place us in Christ, then behavior can't take us out of Christ.

The phrase "in Christ" is seen over and over in scripture. When it is used in reference to a promise, God's grace, redemption, victory, etc... all those things are available to us because we are "in Him." This is why we pray in the name of the Lord Jesus Christ, our prayers are heard because He tore the veil to grant us this access. We are connected to the Father because of our position "in Christ." We are accepted, because we are "in Christ," we are forgiven because we are "in Christ," and we are righteous because we are "in Christ."

> *God made him who had no sin to be sin for us, so that **in him** we might become the righteousness of God.*
> (2 Corinthians 5:21, NIV, emphasis added)

In Christ, we are righteous before God, or right with God as the New Living Translation says it.

> *For God made Christ, who never sinned, to be*

the offering for our sin, **so that we could be made right with God through Christ.**

(2 Corinthians 5:21, emphasis added)

God wants us to remember who we are, and once we grab hold of this truth, we WILL begin developing a lifestyle to match it. We are royal children of God who reflect our Father. Holy. Righteous. Loving.

Since Jesus secured our position of being right with God, am I saying it is a free for all? Forget the rules. Do what we want? It doesn't matter if we sin? I'm glad you asked, because if you hadn't, I would be worried I wasn't accurately sharing the gospel. Because when Paul brought this good news to everyone, this is exactly the question he had to address.

Well then, since God's grace has set us free from the law, does that mean we can go on sinning? Of course not!

(Romans 6:15)

Free for all? I will respond just as Paul did. Of. Course. Not.

Sin is bad. Sin never leads to anything good. Sin brings destruction. Sin steals our identity. When we sin we aren't acting like our true, born anew, righteous self.

Realizing our performance doesn't affect our standing before God is not a license to do anything we want. Sin separates us from experiencing life to the fullest. God didn't restore our position with Him so we could do whatever we want with no consequences. There are natural things which occur when poor decisions are made. I'm sure we've all heard the phrase "you reap what you sow."

Here's a practical example: If someone lies, they will probably have guilt about it and live in constant worry of being found out. There is a good chance the truth will be discovered, and if this happens, people will no longer trust this person. The one who lied may even have to come clean and admit their fault before others, experience public shame, and it could take a long time before anyone will believe them again. God is not punishing this person; their own actions created their reality.

God restored us to a permanent righteous position to free us from a mindset which says we have to strive and perform to please God. Knowing our standing empowers us to live life FREE from the power of sin. When we move from law (performance mentality) to grace (acceptance mentality), sin loses its power. Before we believed in Christ we were bound to our old master: sin. Under grace we are bound to a new leader: Jesus.

Sin is no longer your master, for you no longer live under the requirements of the law. Instead, you live under the freedom of God's grace.

(Romans 6:14)

Grace is what sets Christianity apart from every other religion. Grace is astounding. It is unheard of, unpracticed by the world, and unnatural. The world says you get what you deserve. Grace says you don't get what you deserve, you get what Jesus deserves. *Hallelujah!* We don't "do" to achieve a position. We are freely, graciously, and amazingly given a position, a gift of righteousness. Opening this gift does not lead to more sin, it leads to less.

In the Romans 3 passage we explored in the last chapter, we learned God declares us righteous because through Christ Jesus, He freed us from the penalty for our sins.

> *For everyone has sinned; we all fall short of God's glorious standard. Yet God, with undserved kindness, declares that we are righteous. He did this through Christ Jesus when he freed us from the penalty for our sins.*
> (Romans 3:23-24)

We all have sinned and we all will sin. Everyone on the planet has missed perfection. When a sin is committed, an atonement must be made. I am not talking about asking for forgiveness, I am saying blood must be shed in order for the stain to be removed from our account. Basically, in the spiritual realm, in order to set things right, a penance must be paid to restore what was lost. I'm not sure why it is blood which restores, but this is how God set up the world. From the beginning of time on earth, way back in the garden of Eden, a sacrifice covered the offense. This is where Adam and Eve got those animal skin clothes, the animal had to die in order for them to get their "covering."

Even before creation, God took a look at every sin that would ever be committed and saw there was no sacrifice of any animal or person which could ever cover *all* of humanity's many offenses. He came up with a plan of redemption (we talked about this back in the *Dynamite Love* section). God took the form of a man and became God the Son. The blood flowing through His veins was divine, perfect, and sinless, and could make atonement for the entire human race. Jesus's blood was more than enough to restore.

Glorious Jesus.

Jesus stepped in, sacrificed Himself for every person who would ever live and for those who believe; we've been set free from the penalty of all our sins. The penalty or result of sin is separation from God and spiritual death. But Jesus freed us from this penalty forever. No more separation. Eternal life is ours. While Christ-followers still may sin, it won't separate us because it has already been paid for in advance. We are liberated from that penalty because our faith in Christ has us covered. "Look, the Lamb of God, who TAKES AWAY the sin of the world!" (John 1:29 NIV) Jesus went to the grave and was buried with the sins of the world. But when He rose, the sin stayed buried, never to be credited to us again. To say sin would separate a Christian from God would imply Jesus didn't take them away—they are still hanging around causing a problem between us and the Father.

Did I just ruffle some religious feathers? If I did, let me explain. I know when I first grasped this concept, it did not sound like it could be true. But then I recalled familiar biblical stories of Jesus interacting with the woman at the well (John 4), Zacchaeus (Luke 19), and the woman caught in adultery (John 8). These were people who were flat caught in their sin, and their behavior sure didn't separate them from Jesus. He went right up to them and did not blast them, but instead treated them with dignity. He did not condemn them, but instead had compassion. He showed them love, forgiveness, and reminded them of their worth. This encounter with the gracious, living God is what empowered them to finally leave that lifestyle of sin. This is our God. When we fall, He restores. I used to think when I messed up, I couldn't be in God's presence, but now I know, because of Jesus, I'm completely forgiven of all my past and all my future sins. Now when I sin, the first place I run is His presence to be restored and reminded who I really am. Loved. Seen. Valued. Forgiven.

I love how pastor Steven Furtick shares what our faith in Christ secures for us:

> Your sins and shortcomings don't separate you from God, because he has accepted you through your faith in Jesus. You are preapproved through Jesus, not through your own works or performance.[20]

Everything hangs on Jesus. This is why He's called the cornerstone. In the ancient world, the cornerstone was the most important stone in the building. If it was not level, then the walls would lean and fall as the building was erected. When we say Jesus is our cornerstone, we are declaring that He is the most important thing in our faith and that He is the only immovable foundation on which we stand strong. If we attempt to build our faith on anything else (a denomination, our performance, a ministry, our cause, etc...) it won't be long before our walls come tumbling down, because those foundations are faulty. But not our Savior. He is the cornerstone where the people of God can find everlasting security. It is all about Jesus. Our holiness, our forgiveness, and our righteousness is possible because of our Messiah—the spotless Lamb of God. As believers, our true identity in Christ means we are eternally found in Him. He is the rock of our salvation.

Believing the Good News—we are blameless in the eyes of God the Father because of Jesus—is the foundation from which we stand and must build our lives upon. If we attempt to build a life revolving around our performance, we would find ourselves standing on unstable ground. We must understand as Christ-followers our identity is not that we are fallen and trying to earn good-standing, but instead, we are the redeemed and reinstated children of the Most High. This is important because as we realize who we are, we can tell others who they are—we've got good news for people!

Healthy trees bask in the sun and naturally produce the energy needed to grow through a process called photosynthesis. The leaves soak up sunlight and carbon dioxide to create fats, proteins, and starches which not only feeds the tree itself, but also as a byproduct of the process, oxygen is released into the air. A tree harnesses the sunlight to sustain itself and improve the surrounding environment. Similarly, by standing in our true identity—realizing we are permanently in Christ and living in the light, as He is in the light—we are supernaturally strengthened, not only for our own growth but also for everyone we come in contact with. We've got to tell people God has come for them to restore all that was lost—unending fellowship with the Father because of Jesus. We've got an incredible God and this is amazing news y'all! *Can I get an AMEN?!*

MISSING THE BULLSEYE

I grew up with brothers, which means when they wanted to pick on someone, I was the obvious choice. One birthday my older brother, Tim, got a brand new toy bow and arrow, and who do you think he chose for his target practice? Little ol' me. I remember the sharp sting of the plastic arrow hitting me, and I recall running towards the house to tattle, as all little girls are quick to do. "I'm telling mom!" I shouted over my shoulder as I ran to blow the whistle on his misbehavior. My big bro—who at this point knew he was in trouble—thought he might as well jump all in and have as much fun as he could, and declared, "Oh no you don't!" He drew his arrow and aimed in my direction for one last blow before I reached the front door. *BAM!* It was a direct hit. He hit his mark. What a punk. I still told, but he had his fun and we've laughed about this story again and again. I even shared it during the toast I gave at his wedding.

In the Bible, when you see the word "sin," it actually means "missing the mark." We are supposed to love and live godly lives and when we don't, we miss the bullseye. We all fail at times, whether we're dealing with our own Kryptonite, we are discouraged, or we are just being plain selfish, we miss it. So what then? When God says you are righteous, but you aren't acting that way. Let's see what happens…

My dear children, I am writing this to you so that you will not sin. **But if anyone does sin, we have an advocate who pleads our case before the Father. He is Jesus Christ, the one who is truly righteous.** *He himself is the sacrifice that atones for our sins—and not only our sins but the sins of all the world.*

(1 John 2:1-2, emphasis added)

If I can put this in my own words: we sin, we mess up, we miss the target again and again. And Jesus steps in before Father God for us. I imagine the heavenly conversation going something like this:

"What are they doing now?" God the Father leans over and says to Jesus.

"Yeah, they should have made a better choice, but don't forget they are covered. This one trusts in me. They are under my blood. I've got them. They are wearing my righteousness. It is about what I did, not what they did. I'm interceding on their behalf," Jesus replies.

"Well that is true. But WHY do they keep doing these crazy things?"

"We're working on it, dad."

Phew. Thank you Jesus. The only one who is truly righteous, the only one who could condemn us, the only one who has a right to judge, doesn't. He gives us life—His life. He covers us and fights for us. He has atoned for ALL of our sin for all time. Have faith in Him. He is a good shepherd and a great Lord. Jesus Christ, our Lord, our righteousness.

This is the name he will be called: **The LORD is Our Righteousness.'**
(Jeremiah 23:6b, CSB, emphasis added)

I love this verse because it talks of a time the people of God will declare: *It is Jesus Christ the LORD who is our righteousness*—He is the reason we're right with God. I say the time is now to declare this. When I mess up, I am quick to say "I'm sorry" to God, but I am not returned to my position afterwards, because I never moved in the first place. My performance didn't achieve this righteous position, it doesn't maintain this righteousness, and my performance cannot strip the robe of righteousness off me. Right standing before God has ALWAYS been a gift given to me (and all God's children) because of Jesus's performance. Our behavior did not get us this spot, therefore our behavior cannot remove us from this spot. Our faith must be in our sacrifice, not in our behavior, if we are to live free. Jesus's blood does not stop covering us when we sin—His sacrifice still stands. This was life changing for me.

I have found what helps me the most when I have missed the mark is to declare my position and why I am in that undeserved place. I go ahead and say it out loud.

God made him who had no sin to be sin for us, so that in him we might become the righteousness of God.

(2 Corinthians 5:21, NIV)

I did just mess up, I admit it, I apologize and ask for forgiveness to whom it may concern, God, my husband, my kids, my friends. But I remind myself, the reason my position didn't change, was because I'm right with God not because of *my* actions, but because of *Jesus's* actions. Christ was offered for my sin (all of it). My actions didn't make me righteous; my actions won't make me unrighteous. I am still in Christ and wearing His righteousness.

Evangelist Andrew Wommack teaches about this in his book, *GRACE: The Power of the Gospel.*

You need to understand that when you were born again, your spirit instantly became righteous... After being born again, it is not our nature to sin anymore... Of course, a Christian can commit acts of sin. But what Paul is saying (in Romans 6:20-22) is that just like a lost person's good actions cannot change their sin nature, neither can a born-again believer's sinful actions change their righteous nature... If your acts of righteousness as a lost person couldn't change your sinful nature, then neither can your acts of sin as a Christian change your righteous nature. That's awesome! [21]

Understanding that Jesus eternally covers us, and that our righteous nature doesn't change when we sin results in a people falling more and more in love with our Savior everyday. It makes us focus less on our actions and causes us to celebrate and illuminate what He did. This is similar to what the warmth of the sun does to maple trees in the Spring. When the temperatures fluctuate between freezing at night and rising above zero degrees in the day, sap begins to flow. As the sunlight begins to warm up, the tree signals the roots to soak up more moisture, and the sugar which is stored in the roots move up into the trunk through the sap flow. Understanding what Jesus did for us—focusing on what He did and who our LORD is—signals our roots to dig deeper down into His love.

Realizing we are still counted righteous in God's

eyes, even though we've messed up, draws us deeper in love with our Savior. As we live free from condemnation, we are lifted up to a place where we can actually stop struggling with the same old sin. We need to become less sin-conscious and more Jesus-conscious. It is imperative to always remember we are found forever "in Christ." The more we see ourselves as righteous, the more we start living that way. Just like loved people love people, righteous people live righteously. As Mercy Lokulutu said at the Face 2 Face Women's Conference, "We don't have a behavior problem, we have an identity problem."[22] Until we know what Jesus did and who we truly are, we won't have the full ability to live as the Bible teaches. How we live is in a direct response to how we see ourselves—our identity fuels our behavior.

GIFT EXCHANGE

Growing up, my family didn't have a lot of money. Most of the time our presents were hand-me-downs or bought at a garage sale for cheap, and honestly I did not mind at all. The presents we received may not have been brand new, but they were new to us. One Christmas when I was nine years old, I asked my mom for a doll house I'd seen on TV. She told me we couldn't afford it that year. Knowing this to be true, I understood I would not be getting such an expensive gift. But, on Christmas morning I had a HUGE box under the tree and guess what was inside? The exact doll house I had hoped for. I was truly surprised, and even though I was young, I so appreciated this gift because I knew how my parents must have sacrificed to give me that. It meant so much to me.

I do love gift giving, especially to children. Kids open up their presents with an excitement usually not found in adults. I have three children of my own, so between birthdays and holidays we see our fair share of gift opening.

When my kids tear into their presents, they receive them with joy and are extremely thankful. Let me tell you what NEVER happens though. Not once has one of my kids said, "Oh, mom, I don't deserve this present," or "Dad, please let me go earn some money to pay you back for this." Those thoughts do not even enter my children's minds. They would never try to pay us back and most certainly wouldn't deny a gift. They know the present is for them, they accept their new treasure with giddiness, and then they get to playing. But have you ever been around an adult opening a present who responds with, "Oh you shouldn't have," or, "You didn't need to buy me anything." It's not that adults are unthankful, I think we are just more aware of our faults and often question whether we "deserve" to be celebrated.

Recently, I was thinking about how kids open and receive gifts and how this parallels a truth in the scripture. I thought of how Jesus says people will enter His Kingdom, in Matthew 18:3 (NIV, emphasis added).

*And he said: "Truly I tell you, unless you change and **become like little children**, you will never enter the kingdom of heaven."*

I think a lot of, if not all, Christ followers start off our journey with the Lord with childlike faith—in awe of what He has done and the forgiveness we've received. We are thankful to be connected to God. Like children, we receive the gift of our salvation and forgiveness and right standing with Him joyfully.

Let's take a moment and think about the passion we had when we first entered into a relationship with God—recall what it felt like to be on fire for Him. I remember feeling like someone had lit a blazing bonfire in my soul. I started sharing Christ with everybody. But somewhere along my journey, my focus shifted from what Christ had done to what I was doing. I found myself putting more faith in my performance than in Christ's performance. I was no longer simply receiving the gift of salvation, but striving to earn and sustain God's favor in my life. Some days I wondered if I was acting good enough to get to Heaven and questioned my salvation experience regularly. Can anyone relate?

*For the sin of this one man, Adam, caused death to rule over many. But even greater is **God's wonderful grace and his gift of righteousness,** for all who receive it will live in triumph over sin and death through this one man, Jesus Christ.*
(Romans 5:17, emphasis added)

The Bible says for all who *receive* God's grace

and gift of righteousness will triumph over sin and death through Christ. It does not say all who *earn* God's grace and righteousness. We cannot perform to be under God's grace and we cannot earn His gift of righteousness, we can only receive them both. This was HUGE for me to grasp, and when I did, I was never the same.

Grace *and* righteousness are unearned. How we started our journey with God is how we are supposed to walk it out every day of our lives—continually receiving salvation as a gift. And look at the result of receiving as a gift this grace and right standing before God by faith: *triumph over sin and death, through Christ.*

We all want to live this life well. And I think we are VERY aware of all the changes we need to make. But victory will not come by focusing on our faults. Triumph comes by fixing our eyes on our Savior, believing what He did for us, and accepting our new position as a glorious gift.

> ***Therefore, since we have been made right in God's sight by faith, we have peace with God because of what Jesus Christ our Lord has done for us.*** *Because of our faith, Christ has brought us into this place of undeserved privilege where we now stand, and we confidently and joyfully look forward to sharing God's glory.*
> (Romans 5:1-2, emphasis added)

Isn't this scripture amazing?! We have peace with

God *right now*—not one day when we get to Heaven. We are made right with God the moment we decide to place our faith in Jesus. In Judah Smith's book *Life Is___*, He makes this incredible connection:

> God had promised that one day he would make a covenant of peace with his people. One day peace would be restored. In the book of Isaiah, chapter 54, God declared to Israel, "For the mountains shall depart and the hills be removed, but My kindness shall not depart from you, nor shall My covenant of peace be removed" (v.10). Now, Jesus was telling his disciples that this covenant of peace had arrived. They could have shalom with God and shalom in life not through keeping the law, but through Jesus... The Ten Commandments couldn't save us and didn't save us and won't save us. We trust in Jesus, to do for us what we could not do for ourselves... We find our peace in his peformance and perfection... Our righteousness is established and peace is restored. Jesus is the way to peace with God... Without Jesus, we have no righteousness and therefore no shalom. But through him, we can enjoy true peace.[23]

We have peace with God because of what someone else (Jesus) did. Doesn't that just sound too good to be true? This is grace. And this is why it is called amazing, because it is almost unbelievable that we actually are at peace with God because of Jesus. Jesus is amazing. The scripture we just read (Romans 5:2) also says:

> *Because of our faith, Christ has brought us into this place of undeserved privilege where we now stand, and we confidently and joyfully look forward to sharing God's glory.*

Thank you Jesus! He brought us into a place of undeserved privilege. This is grace. The Son of God, our Messiah, brought us into this new, unearned position. Living right with God is a whole new world. Having peace with God is an entirely new level of rest. His righteousness brings us confidence and boldness. It fills us with joy. Back in the day, when I was self-righteous, I was only confident on the days I performed well. Now I place my hope in Christ's performance, in His righteousness, and He makes me brave every day.

Jesus is our unshakeable advocate before the Father. Because His righteousness is unmovable, like a mighty mountain, we can always bank our standing with God on His perfect performance. He is such a faithful, good, powerful Lord.

DIGGING DEEPER

Listen to "Cornerstone," by Hillsong Worship.

Read Ephesians 2:8-9, 14-20.

1. What is a time in your life where God showed you grace instead of condemnation? How did you feel?

2. How is the way you deal with your short-comings and mistakes different than the way God does?

3. What can you do when you miss the mark to act less like an orphan and more like one who has been made righteous through the sacrifice of Jesus?

9

ROYAL TREATMENT

Have you ever seen the movie *The Princess Diaries*? It is such a great story of a girl named Mia: a frumpy teenager who is unnoticed, clumsy, and does not consider herself special. Until she finds out one day that she actually is very special. She meets her grandmother for the first time who is a queen, and discovers that she is, in fact, a princess. Mia had always been royal, she just didn't know it. She was born into this position, but because she was totally unaware, she didn't act like a princess.

Just like Mia, as followers of Christ, we were also born into a new position, only some of us didn't know it. The moment we accepted Jesus as our Savior and chose to follow Him, we became a new creation, regenerated by God's Spirit. We were born anew, righteous. God Himself declares it (Romans 2:24). So why do we not always act righteously? Why do we still have faults? Just like the princess who was clueless she was royalty, so we too are often unaware of our position. Jesus secured our place before God. Just like Mia didn't have to act like a princess to become one, we didn't act right righteous to become so. Once Mia found out she was a princess, she started the training to act like one. Now that you know God calls you righteous, and you are in that position because of Jesus's work on the cross, not your work, your life will start reflecting it.

> *When Adam sinned, sin entered the world. Adam's sin brought death, so death spread to everyone, for everyone sinned... But there is a great difference between Adam's sin and God's gracious gift. For the sin of this one man, Adam, brought death to many. But even greater is God's wonderful grace and his gift of forgiveness to many through this other man, Jesus Christ. And the result of God's gracious gift is very different from the result of that one man's sin. For Adam's sin led to condemnation, **but God's free gift leads to our being made right with God, even though we are guilty of many sins.***
>
> (Romans 5:12, 15-16, emphasis added)

When Adam fell, his sinful nature was passed down to every human that would ever be born. *That kind of stinks.* So, from birth we naturally sin, because what Adam did was credited to all of the human race. But when Jesus came, all our sins were imputed to Him at the cross. He dealt with the sin and paid the price once and for all. Now, because of the cross, Jesus's righteousness is credited to all who claim Him as Lord. *That totally rocks!*

What the Romans passage we just read is saying is what Jesus did was greater than what Adam did. You see, what Adam did could be undone. What Jesus did cannot be undone. *Can I get an Amen?!* The pressure to perform and gain approval is debilitating. Our faith has got to be in Jesus. We must believe His blood covers us for all time and that He is enough to bridge the gap to God forever; That He is the Lamb of God who took away all of our sins. AND, we are NO longer under condemnation because we are in Christ.

> *When he sees all that is accomplished by his anguish, he will be satisfied. And because of his experience, **my righteous servant will make it possible for many to be counted righteous,** for he will bear all their sins.*
> (Isaiah 53:11, emphasis added)

Jesus bore all our sins, so we could be counted righteous. We aren't righteous because we always act that way, we are counted righteous because Jesus acted that way and He traded spots with us. It is not about what we do, it's about what He did. His identity is now our identity because we are united with Christ.

RISE AND SHINE

I like my sleep. My husband likes his sleep. So naturally we thought our children would love to sleep. Before having my first child, Drew, I was CONVINCED he would sleep through the night early on, because surely he would take after one of his parents. *Ha!* I laugh because Drew did sleep through the night, eventually, and by eventually I mean after he turned one year old! And his siblings followed in suit. Not only did they rise frequently throughout the night, they also rose early (and are still early risers). It doesn't matter what time my sweet ones go to bed, they will be getting up at 7 am—or earlier. (Can I just take this moment to pose the question: WHY do I have to drag my children out of bed on a school day, but come vacation they are ready to go at 6 am? Now that ain't right!) Anyway, all that to say this mama had to learn real quick to rise and shine with the sun. I do rise, but as far as the "shine" part, let's just say I get there eventually, after my coffee. #notamorningperson

Rising. Getting up. Advancing. Ascending. Mounting up. Growing. This is the legacy of the God's children. Look at the process described in Proverbs:

> *For though the righteous fall seven times, they rise again, but the wicked stumble when calamity strikes.*
> (Proverbs 24:16, NIV)

Notice the verbs used to describe a righteous person. Rising *and* falling. Though a righteous person falls, they rise again. Does the fall make a person unrighteous? No. This verse points out that a righteous person does in fact fall. But it doesn't end in the fall. They rise again. *Amen!* This is our heritage as the righteousness of God in Christ… we *will* stumble, but because we are in Christ and our position hasn't changed, we will find our footing again and stand firm. We do not and cannot fall out of Christ.

If we can get a hold of this — believing we are forevermore in a position we can't lose, we will live in freedom. This section is called shattering light, because as we step into the light of who we are in Christ, that illumination shatters the dark shadow sin casts. This is the brilliance of gospel that we need to own. When we are walking in this truth, we become a beacon of light to the world.

> *But for you who fear my name, the Sun of Righteousness will rise with healing in his wings. And you will go free, leaping with joy like calves let out to pasture.*
>
> (Malachi 4:2)

The Sun of Righteousness is Jesus. His light is illuminating the only path we can take to be right with God. The truth about our awesome Savior is rising over us to set us free from performing, earning, and striving. There is healing for our souls and bodies, and it starts with us established in His righteousness. As we step into the sun and see ourselves clothed in Christ, we will rise and shine as royal children of light.

For you were once darkness, but now you are light in the Lord. Live as children of light.
(Ephesians 5:8, NIV)

FILL UP THE TANK

We are a spontaneous family. Let me give you a glimpse of what I mean. Once, my husband called me at 11:00 am and posed the question: "Hey, you want to go to Florida today?" We had not been discussing Florida. We had not saved up for a trip. We had nothing packed. But, do you know what my love-for-adventure-self said? "Heck yes!" And I kid you not, we were on the road by two o'clock that afternoon. We had no plans, but we figured it out on the way. It was one of the best trips we've had, and we would do it again in a heartbeat.

Most of us have taken an epic road trip, or at least have had a memorable one. So imagine with me for a moment we are putting together this amazing cross country expedition. We have the course mapped out. We have all the food stops planned (thank you very much Yelp for making all my foodie dreams come true). We know the sights we want to see, and we even left ourselves some margin in case some unplanned adventure pops up. We are packed. We are in the driveway, and we're ready to leave. We are about to burst at the seams with excitement because we know this trip is going to be flippin' awesome. Now, it is time, we push start on our GPS app, turn the key to get this party started and the engine roars to life. We position the gear into drive and push down on the pedal to go. The car moves slightly, sputters a little, then dies. And it is then the realization hits: in all these preparations to do something great, we forgot an essential step of the process: making sure our tank was full of gas. We aren't going anywhere. No matter how hard we've planned, how much research we've done, how many pins we've pinned on Pinterest, we will not be doing ANY of those things because we have no fuel to get us there!

Fuel is kind of a big deal. Without it, you won't make any headway, no matter how much you know, how much you've read, or how much you've prepped. You cannot drive on an empty tank of gas. You need to power your vehicle to make this stellar trip happen.

Life is like that. We have all these plans, right? We want to do big things for God. We want to love well and live well and do right. But we get stuck. We want to be on fire. We want to be a part of a great adventure. We want to be obedient. We want to change the world. But without the right fuel it is hard to get moving, or if we get a little something going, we get burned out fast because we are running on fumes—our own strength—and not the actual thing.

Knowing Jesus and our position in Him is the fuel which enables us to grow into who we are meant to be. Once we see ourselves the way God sees us, our actions will begin to align with the teachings of the Bible.

We are made right with God through our Savior and no other way. As much as some of us would like to have something to do with it, we cannot earn a righteous position. Even our best attempts would fall short. Jesus clothed us in His own righteousness so we could once again be united with the Father, like Adam and Eve were before The Fall. This position was earned by our Savior and given as gift to His followers. When we come to the light of our unearned—but secure—identity in Christ it fuels the growth process in us. When we see ourselves the way God does, as truly righteous, our lives will change dramatically and we will take this show on the road. Knowing how we look to God fuels us for the ride of our lives.

In Revelation, John prophesies about a time when God's church is going to look beautiful. When we will be filled with His love, rejoicing together, unified and dazzling. Check it out:

> *Let us be glad and rejoice, and give honour to him: for the marriage of the Lamb is come, and his wife hath made herself ready. And **to her was granted that she should be arrayed in fine linen, clean and white: for the fine linen is the righteousness of saints.***
>
> (Revelation 19:7-8, KJV, emphasis added)

And the bride wore white. She was dressed in righteousness granted to her to wear. This is the robe of righteousness—given to us by God. This verse is not saying, "Oh the saints of God finally got their act together and began behaving right." This verse refers to a future time when the followers of Christ embrace the truth that the ONLY way to be right with God is through the blood of Jesus, which makes us white as snow, and justified before the Father.

What if the church collectively put on His righteousness, and realized we're all actually wearing white? What if we all based our standing before God on Jesus's blood? What a beautiful bride and a mighty army we would be. The nit-picking about whose way is the right way (to dress, worship, preach, do outreach, baptize, etc…) would be eliminated. We'll all point to the only way as Christ.

> *Jesus told him, "I am the way, the truth, and the life. No one can come to the Father except through me."*
> (John 14:6)

Jesus is truly our Lord. By placing our faith in Him for our righteous standing and acceptance before the Lord, we are on a solid rock. That is when we will be immovable and flourishing, like MIGHTY trees, which continually glorify our great God. Remember those great oaks from my childhood home I shared about? Look how the prophet Isaiah describes believers who are planted by God in His righteousness:

> *In their righteousness, they will be like great oaks that the LORD has planted for his own glory.*
>
> (Isaiah 61:3b)

This righteousness is not "our righteous acts," or based on our performance. Our best attempts to act right could never be and will never be enough to sustain our position before God. The only firm foundation we can grow securely upon is the righteousness of God, the position which was earned by Jesus and was given to us to stand in. It is time we lay down our works and point to His. Only His righteousness is good enough. No style of worship we practice, dress code we follow, food or drink we intake, Bible translation we read from, denominational rules we adhere to, church methods we use, nor anything we "do" makes us right with God, JESUS—and only JESUS—is the reason we are counted righteous.

In speaker John Bevere's book, *The Holy Spirit,* he highlights what stands out about each person of the Godhead, and when he shares about Jesus, he says,

> As believers, we must never forget our right standing with God—which is the very cornerstone of this amazing relationship with the Spirit—would have never been possible if it were not for the grace of

our Lord and Savior, Jesus Christ. This grace cannot be earned or merited; it is the great gift of His life, which includes forgiveness, redemption, and empowerment.[24]

Knowing you are right with God produces obedience, not the other way around. We don't act a certain way to get accepted, loved, and to get right with God, we already are all these things by Jesus's finished work of the cross (this is just a fancy way of saying: what Jesus accomplished on the cross for us). Our Savior bought more than our ticket to heaven; He purchased our freedom, gave us access to the tree of life, redemption, acceptance, righteousness, holiness, and much more. What a king! Jesus is known as the King of kings. As we embrace this new royal position, we begin to reign over the things of this world, instead of letting them rule over us. This was always God's intention for humanity (Genesis 1:28).

Stepping into the light of this revelation of our true identity "in Christ," and becoming one with our awesome Savior, shatters the lies of darkness, setting us on fire, to be the light of the world.

HE IS JESUS, MY SAVIOR & KING
I AM RIGHTEOUS IN CHRIST

DIGGING DEEPER

Listen to "What A Beautiful Name," by Hillsong Worship.

Read Acts 13:39.

1. What are some things you can do to practically remind yourself that you are righteous and royal every day?

2. What chains can be broken in your mind by knowing you are forever in a place of righteousness and royalty in Christ?

3. How do you think the body of Christ would become more unified if we all recognized our righteous standing is based solely on Jesus and celebrated it in each other?

THERE IS ONE WHO CAN BRING MORE PURPOSE, DIRECTION, EMPOWERMENT, AND COMFORT THAN WE'VE EVER KNOWN. HE IS GOD'S OWN SPIRIT, AND WE'RE MEANT TO WALK THROUGH LIFE WITH HIM AS OUR MAGNIFICENT GUIDE AND HELPER. HE GIVES US THIS BURSTING-AT-THE-SEEMS LIFE WE LONG FOR, AND AS WE STEP INTO HIS OVERFLOWING RIVER WE ARE FOREVER CHANGED, REFRESHED, AND POSITIONED TO REACH OUR FULLEST POTENTIAL.

OVERFLOWING LIFE

THE SPIRIT OF GOD, WHO RAISED JESUS FROM THE DEAD, LIVES IN YOU. AND JUST AS GOD RAISED CHRIST JESUS FROM THE DEAD, HE WILL GIVE LIFE TO YOUR MORTAL BODIES BY THIS SAME SPIRIT LIVING WITHIN YOU.

ROMANS 8:11

10

CONNECT TO THE SOURCE

When I lived in Michigan, I discovered that something really spectacular happens when spring arrives in the Mitten State. The snow and ice thaw, leaving a muddy, soggy mess everywhere you look (hang in there we're getting to the good part). But it doesn't stay that way. There is a purpose for all the moisture, and as it seeps down into the earth it provides the water needed for new growth to sprout and rejuvenate the land. Once the warm sunlight combines with the moist earth, it causes the flowers to burst open and, together with the carpet of new, lush, green grass, announces the arrival of the long-awaited season of new beginnings.

During my time in Michigan, I developed a new appreciation for the spring season and all the flourishing plant life which appears each year. The rain is steady, leaving the land well-watered and thriving. After those May showers, the spring fades into summer and this season is as mild and beautiful there as the winters are harsh. If one can just make it through the ice and crazy Michigan snow storms, there are some glorious months on the way. In contrast, growing up in the southern part of the states, I experienced some brutally HOT summers where the sunlight was plentiful, and at times the rainfall was scarce. Without any steady snow-fall to prep the ground with an extra supply of moisture to endure the scorching heat, the lack of rain often resulted in droughts. I remember the water restrictions put into place to preserve the precious commodity of limited water, and everyone's yards took a visible hit. This affected me because I typically ran around barefoot all summer and, let me tell you, dry, dead, crunchy grass is no friend to a shoe-less little girl. It's a sad fact: without water, things die.

The Holy Spirit is often referred to as living water, rivers of water, water of life. We can set our roots into the love of a Good Father, we can come to the light of the gos-pel and our identity of being righteous in Christ alone, but if these truths aren't watered by the power of the Holy Spirit, we dry up. Trees that aren't well-watered become suscep-tible to diseases and insect problems, lose their coloring, shrivel up, and in extreme cases, will die. Plants need water to not only survive but thrive. Similarly, in order to be a healthy, well balanced person, it is of utmost importance we get acquainted with the Spirit of God. Remember, knowing all three sides of God is imperative to a life that thrives, re-sembling those strong trees.

In my opinion, the Holy Spirit is the least talked about side of God, especially considering all the things He is called: our counselor, helper, comforter, teacher, guide, reminder, the one who empowers, the voice of God, His presence.

One REALLY interesting thing about God's Spirit is that He is the game changer between the Old Covenant and the New Covenant. Under the "old way" God's people were to follow the law. But under the "new way" Christ followers are to follow the Spirit. To teach, understand, and walk under the new covenant of grace must be done with the Holy Spirit's help.

> *He has enabled us to be ministers of his new covenant. This is a covenant not of written laws, **but of the Spirit**. The old written covenant ends in death; **but under the new covenant, the Spirit gives life**. The old way, with laws etched in stone, led to death, though it began with such glory that the people of Israel could not bear to look at Moses' face. For his face shone with the glory of God, even though the brightness was already fading away. Shouldn't we expect far greater glory under the new way, now that the **Holy Spirit is giving life**?*
> (2 Corinthians 3: 6-11, emphasis added)

The Old Covenant at its simplest says you have to perform to be right with God. But the problem is people can't consistently obey. God saw that *any* covenant based on people's actions wasn't going to work. While He is ALWAYS faithful on His end, we aren't on ours. The reason the old way led to death was because every failed attempt to follow the rules perfectly resulted in condemnation. Being constantly conscious of failure brings guilt and destruction. And the sin itself brings death and decay. Don't get me wrong, the Old Covenant had its place. However, it was never the solution, but instead pointed out our great need for a Savior. So God made a New Covenant. A fresh promise. A better way. This New Covenant would lead to life, because now we don't relate to God based on our performance, but rather through what Jesus did for us. Rules don't lead to life, living in the Spirit does.

But now we have been released from the law, for we died to it and are no longer captive to its power. Now we can serve God, not in the old way of obeying the letter of the law, but in the new way of living in the Spirit.

(Romans 7:6)

Living "in the Spirit" is the new way. When we live in step with God the Holy Spirit, we finally *can* serve Him. In fact, it is the only way we can walk our Christian life successfully. We all have the Holy Spirit living within us if Christ is our Lord. But just because you have something doesn't mean you are utilizing it.

A few years back it was unusually hot. I was still

living in Michigan and we were having a heat wave. It was 100 degrees in September! Now this temperature is hot no matter where you are, but in Michigan it was a total anomaly, especially since we were one month away from the arrival of snow, possibly—you never know what the weather is going to do in Michigan. During this "heat wave" I was sweating just walking around my house, and when I checked out the thermostat, I discovered the room temperature was 80 degrees at 8 o'clock at night. What puzzled me is that it was set at 71 degrees. So I did the rundown, made sure it was on, set to cool, and fan running. But nothing was changing. We'd just had our air conditioner worked on so I knew it wasn't broken, but yet, there I was in a pool of sweat. Finally, I opened up the utility closet and discovered the power was switched to "off" on the air unit. I flipped it to "on" and it roared to life. Suddenly, a wind of fresh cool air started circulating through our home. #Ahhhhhhh

The cool air had always been available, but it wasn't connected to power, so I wasn't benefiting from it. I had it, but I wasn't utilizing it. Similarly, the Holy Spirit has always been available, but perhaps we haven't known how to connect to His power. Knowing God as Spirit connects us to the power to walk fully in our purpose and live a life on fire for the Lord.

This "new way," this glorious life-to-the-fullest that Jesus talked about, can only be fully comprehended and walked out with the help of the Holy Spirit. To follow Him and live in step with Him, we have to know the Spirit of God intimately. So, let's dive into the living water that brings unending and overflowing life.

THE APPLE DOESN'T FALL FAR

I have three children: Drew, Emma, and Jack. They are sweet and funny and amazing, but lest you think I lead a calm life, I must confess that parenting these three is the biggest adventure I've ever known. Every time something crazy is going down, I am able to hold it together (usually) by telling myself: *Okay. Just breath mama. This may be straight up nuts right now, but keep in mind, this will probably make a good story to tell one day.* Because boring, non-eventful families have no stories to relive and laugh hysterically at. I have stories y'all. Many, many, stories. (God apparently knew I was going to be a writer, and He most certainly made sure I would NEVER run out of material.)

One of the craziest things about being a parent is seeing myself in my kids. Children typically act a whole lot like their parents. Most of us are familiar with the saying, "Do as I say, not as I do." Well, we can just forget that— more than likely this is not happening. Typically kids will do as their parents do. At least that has been my experience. Just like a tree replicates itself (it produces fruit filled with seeds, releases them to the ground, the seed takes root and sprouts up into another tree), so the fruit present in a parent is often replicated in their children. The apple doesn't fall far from the tree.

One time, we were walking in the mall as a family, and my husband declares, "I'll be right back." He ran off and started talking to a complete stranger. Afterwards, I said "What was that about?" I was thinking maybe it was an old high school buddy. Oh no, it was a stranger. "Well I felt like God was saying, 'Invite him to church,' as he passed by. So I did." And a few days later, my son Drew took a cue from his daddy and did the same thing. He and I ran an errand which just happened to involve buying delicious Girl Scout cookies. Afterwards we got back in the car, he turned to me and said:

"Mama, I have a feeling I'm supposed to invite them (a mom and daughter) to church."

So of course I backed him, "Go for it baby."

He wasn't sure about stepping out. "I'm a little nervous, will you just do it?"

I knew Drew was scared, but I couldn't let him miss this experience by me taking over, so I told him I would help. "I'll go with you, but I think if you just say exactly what God put in your heart, it will be okay. Plus, if you will do what He asks, He'll give you the words to say. He always does."

So, we did it together. My heart about burst. He said exactly what he had told me and we invited them to spend Easter with us. Sure enough, they weren't planning on attending anywhere. I don't know if they ended up coming, but I prayed they felt loved and that a seed was planted by my Drew. Precious.

Children. They sure do take after their parents.

God calls us His children, and we become more like Him as we get acquainted and walk in step with His Spirit. With the help of the Holy Spirit we begin resembling our Father, doing as He would do, and loving who He would love. One of the Holy Spirit's purposes in our lives is to testify that we are the children of God, and He leads us to look more like children of God.

> *For all who are led by the Spirit of God are children of God. So you have not received a spirit that makes you fearful slaves. Instead, you received God's Spirit when he adopted you as his own children. Now we call him, "Abba, Father." For his Spirit joins with our spirit to affirm that we are God's children.*
> (Romans 8:14-16)

The Spirit of God is a Helper meant to lead us into the great things God has in store for us. The more we follow His leading, the more we will look like a child of God. We already are His children. Jesus purchased our position as a son or daughter of God, but the more we walk in step with God's Holy Spirit, the more our heart aligns with His and the more we resemble our Heavenly Father.

I THOUGHT SO

Let's talk about texting. I actually love communicating through text messages. Texts can be brief, to the point, no fluff, and allow us to access people quickly without interrupting anyone's plans. But there is one tricky side of texts: you can't hear the tone of how something is said. Have you ever received a text message and been unsure how to take it? Possibly it left you thinking, *Wonder what they meant by that?* If we misinterpret the tone or the facial expression of the person who wrote the message, It. Is. Over.

Or, have you ever sent an email or text and got no immediate response? Or possibly you've made a comment and while replaying the moment later on thought, *Oh, no. WHY did I say that?! What are they thinking? I shouldn't have said that. Should I write them a message and just clear the air? They probably think I'm horrible now. I should have just been quiet...*

Only to find out after all your deliberating, your friend finally responds, "Oh, sorry, I forgot to respond, LOL too funny." *Phew.*

Tell me I'm not the only one who has created a catastrophic event in my mind and discovered later all was in fact well the whole time?!

Our thoughts, though. They can get crazy. We make up entire stories and scenarios which most of the time aren't remotely close to the truth. But when there is no immediate response and we are left alone with our thoughts, we can easily imagine the worst.

Our mind is where most battles we face take place. They start there. Well, God's heart is for you to have a mind at peace and to think the way He thinks. But how can we even begin to know God's thoughts?

> *No one can know a person's thoughts except that person's own spirit, and no one can know God's thoughts except God's own Spirit.*
> (1 Corinthians 2:11)

The Holy Spirit knows God's thoughts, and He lives within us. Now I'm not so presumptuous as to say we can know what God is thinking. His ways and thoughts are higher than ours. But I do believe we can allow God's Spirit inside of us to begin changing the way *we* think into the way God thinks. Every believer, the moment they called on Jesus to be their Lord and believed in Him to be their Messiah, became the dwelling place of God's Spirit.

> *And when you believed in Christ, he identified you as his own by giving you the Holy Spirit, whom he promised long ago.*
> (Ephesians 1:13b)

So, the Holy Spirit knows God's thoughts, and we were given Him. God's own Spirit lives inside of us. So how do we tap into and begin thinking the way God thinks? How do we align our thoughts with His? We tap into the Holy Spirit. And how do we do that? We get to know the Holy Spirit and we ask God for help with this.

In his book, *The Holy Spirit,* speaker John Bevere says:

> If we a want deep, intimate relationship with God, we have to know Him by His Spirit. Only the Spirit knows and reveals the thoughts, feelings, and purposes of God's heart.[25]

So if we're to get to know God deeper than ever before, a great place to start is by pursuing the Holy Spirit more. But how do we know when it *is* the Holy Spirit leading or speaking and not our own thoughts? We learn to listen and become familiar with His voice.

JUST SAY YES

"God ONLY speaks through scripture." I'm thankful I was never told this growing up. Oh I've heard it a few times in my adult life, but I respectfully disagree. Why? Because I've heard Him speak, and it changed me forever. There are few voices that can do this. I recall the exact moment, as if it were yesterday, I first heard that still, small whisper, and it was not speaking a Bible verse—but it *was* the voice of God.

My youth group attended the Christian youth camp

"Eighty-six hours" every summer. It was put on by Wisdom Works, lead by Mark Matlock. That week was the highlight of my year! Now, I'll be honest, in my teens I was a tad boy-crazy. (What young girl isn't?!) And camp was always full of hot guys who loved Jesus. It was like the dating-jack-pot for a young Christian girl. (As you can see I started out loving camp for *very* spiritual reasons—insert the laughing with tears emoji.)

I was sixteen and it was Thursday, the worship night at camp. The band *Forty Days* was leading the music and we were praising our little hearts out. As I sang, a calm voice interrupted the moment, "You think you came here to meet a guy, but you're *really* here to meet me." It was God. I had never heard His voice before, but somehow it was so familiar, like I had known it my whole life. In one moment, I went from seeking a guy to being sought by the God of the universe, and I was overwhelmed. I was completely undone with the thought, *This God is for real, and He wants me to meet Him?!* In one instant, I was changed forever, He was no longer my family's God, He was mine. My desires were completely and wholly altered in an instant as my life took a dramatic turn. A fire was forged in my heart that night, and the flame has never gone out. Only the voice of the living God could have brought this kind of change.

If I had been taught God only speaks in Bible vers-es, I would not have been open to hearing from Him in the way I did. I would have disregarded the whisper and who knows when my relationship would have become real? God spoke the earth into existence, He has spoken to His people throughout history, and if He is the same yesterday, today, and forever, how could I ever believe as soon as the Apostle John penned the final words of Revelation He'd decided to stop talking? There is no way. He still speaks to people who are willing to listen, and I say this because I've experienced it. We're designed to hear from our God. Even Jesus said,

> *No! The Scriptures say, 'People do not live by bread alone, but by **every word that comes from the mouth of God.**'*
> (Matthew 4:4)

Jesus did not say, "*came* from the mouth of God," but instead said, "*comes* from the mouth of God." God is still speaking, and I believe He is willing to speak to us through His Spirit. All it takes on our part is to have an open heart to receive the way He desires to connect with us. It is important to understand that the Holy Spirit communicates differently with each of us. I have personally experienced this (and it is displayed throughout the Bible). God connects with people through dreams, prayers, visions, speaking, ideas, scripture verses, and by giving a strong sense of knowing what to do.

It took me a few years to realize the voice I heard when I was sixteen was the Holy Spirit. I knew it was God, but I was unfamiliar with the role of His Spirit. A few years ago, a desire rose in me to hear that familiar voice again, and more frequently—but how? How would I know if it really was God or my own thoughts? As I pressed in to hear the voice of the Holy Spirit a friend gave me some timely advice. "When you hear that voice or nudge, prompting you to do something good, act on it. The more you follow His leading, the louder His voice will become."

I decided to test that out and it has proven to be true.

Here are a few things to keep in mind when learning to discern the voice of the Holy Spirit.

- It will be a good thing.
- It will line up with what the Bible teaches.
- It will be within your ability, but it may not necessarily be in within your comfort zone. (Because let's face it, we don't usually come up with uncomfortable ideas for ourself!)

The Holy Spirit would not do otherwise. He is the Spirit of God and leads only in the will of God.

When I embarked on this journey of saying "yes" to the Spirit of the Lord, I prayed: *God, I want to hear your voice. I am going to try to act on the next thing You tell me. I want to hear the Holy Spirit better. I want to know you and listen more.* I made sure I said "try" because I wanted to be sure I had an "out," in case I was too nervous. True story. I didn't know what He was going to tell me to do.

Well, I remember the day He spoke. I knew it was His voice. It was a good thing, but it was a hard thing. He never said it would be easy. In fact, if it is a difficult, uncomfortable thing, that is a pretty big sign that it likely is Him. Because why would we have the idea to do something out of our comfort zone?! And I would just like to say right here, if you are unsure, seek further, wise counsel. Always be led in peace. You may be nervous, but if it is God, you will have supernatural confidence provided by His Spirit.

Here is what happened. I was visiting a friend who recently had a baby and she was STRUGGLING. She had a pinched nerve in her neck and could barely turn her head. Her hospital experience hadn't been great, she had a terrible headache, and was in a lot of pain. I felt awful for her and wished I knew how to help. We had been friends for a while, she knew I went to church but I rarely talked about God. I didn't want to be pushy or offend her. But just then, God whispered something to my heart.

"I want you to pray with her."

I was not so sure, so of course I resisted. *What? I can't do that. What if she gets mad at me?*

"You said you were going to try to do the next thing I told you."

I said try.

"Are you going to do this or not?"

Okay, fine. Yes, I'll do it.

I desired to hear His voice, walk in step with His Spirit, and know Him more than anything. So I relented. I stepped out of my circle of comfort and took a leap into the unknown.

I asked my friend if it would be okay if prayed for

her. And she said yes! I couldn't believe it. I put my hands on her shoulder and prayed for healing and peace and for things to get better. And then she started to cry.

What?? I was shocked and in awe of what God was doing. Afterwards she thanked me for caring enough to pray for her!! It was incredible, and I am so thankful I crossed the "chicken line," listening to God's voice that day and following His leading.

This experience introduced me to a whole new way of living: listening and acting on the voice of the Holy Spirit. It has taken me on many adventures with God, and I've grown to know and enjoy Him more and more through every situation. The more we listen and say yes, the more we see Him work and the more we know Him. Listening is crucial to knowing.

> *My sheep listen to my voice; I know them, And*
> *they follow me.*
> (John 10:27, NIV)

Listening to his voice and tapping into His Spirit speaking will lead you to know God deeper. There is always further to go with God. He'll whisper truth to you, guide you in decisions, and lead you to do some pretty crazy amazing stuff which gives you a glimpse into His heart. The more you hear Him and say yes, the closer you get in your relationship with Him. And as I've heard it said, "If you want to get closer to God, just do the next thing He says."

Saying yes to God, and letting His Spirit lead me has revealed more of His heart by having me encounter and impact the people He cares about. Partnering with Him continually shows me how awesome He is. He's so good, caring, loving, and often ministers to the unlikely and over-looked. What a God!

Just. Say. Yes.

DIGGING DEEPER

Listen to "Come Holy Spirit," by Vertical Worship.

Read John 6:63.

1. What is your experience with hearing the voice of God? How comfortable are you with His Holy Spirit speaking to you?

2. Has God ever asked you to do something out of your comfort zone? Did you shy away from it or step out in bravery?

3. Where in your life is God asking you to step out in faith and say "yes" to what He is doing in you?

11

GIVE AND TAKE

Once I started tuning into the Holy Spirit's voice, life got REAL interesting. One time, He prompted me to bring bread to a complete stranger's house. This wasn't a meal chain, friend of a friend, or anything. I had NO idea who lived there, but I knew He had led me, so I went. Here's the back story. I had seen a balloon announcing: "It's a girl" as I passed this particular house on my daily walk. A few days later the Spirit prompted me to bring them something to eat to bless them. By this time I had said "yes" enough and had seen Him work so much I knew it was the Spirit leading me. I had a choice to make: say yes and trust He would go with me and give me the right words, or say no, doubt Him, and possibly miss out on a great adventure. I decided on trust and adventure.

And I went.

I had with me my bakery-bought loaf of bread (because who's going to be comfortable eating a homemade food item from a complete stranger, I'm just sayin'). On the way I kept asking God, *Okay, what do I even say to these people?* All the while trusting He loved me and wouldn't send me to a crazy person's house. Just being real.

God replied calm and cool as ever, "I'll tell you when you get there."

So, having no prepared speech I took my food and kids with me to the door. #awkward When the mom came to the door, I opened my mouth to speak and God met me there. "Hey, I know this may sound a little odd, but I just really felt like God was leading me to come and bring you this bread and meet you." And God did the rest.

Turns out they were Christians, they had just started a church, and as of that morning had ran out of bread. *Come on now!* We've been friends ever since. God is something else!

I share this story, because we can sabotage ourselves if we think everything needs to be figured out and planned perfectly before we make a move, but that is not the way God works. He has sent His Spirit to help us, but if we have everything under control, what does He need to do? You don't have to have every speech planned, the prayer rehearsed, the right answers for every question ready. If you trust and rely on the Lord, He shows up when you need Him and does what only He can. Sometimes we only need to be willing to talk, and He'll do the rest.

For it was I, the LORD your God, who rescued

you from the land of Egypt. Open your mouth wide, and I will fill it with good things.
(Psalm 81:10)

I don't know what I am going to say half the time He prompts me to act, but one thing I do know, if I will just open up my mouth, He'll fill it with good words. He has never let me down. He. Is. Faithful.

AS THE WIND BLOWS

Got another movie reference for you. I'm sorry, I just can't help myself. I told you, we are movie people. I mean doesn't everyone know that when faced with a huge life choice, just turn on a Disney movie? I'm sure they have a scenario or song that has just the right answer.

You know what I am talking about. In *Beauty and the Beast,* we're reminded to not judge someone too quickly, and in the song "Tale as Old as Time," we learn it is okay to be wrong and just change. Make those changes, apologize and start again. Happy ending. Thank you, Disney.

Or, how about the truth that love can really change a person? In *Tangled*, Flynn Rider sure makes some big changes after falling in love with Rapunzel. No more stealing for him; he doesn't want to since his heart has been changed. Not to mention he's about the richest guy in the land because his wife is the princess... who needs to steal now?! Right on, Disney.

And they once again hit the nail on the head with my girl Elsa. How could we ever forget the poignant reminder to move beyond our past from the Ice Queen? She tells us to just let it go, break free from the pain of our past and be ourselves. #preachitsista

This isn't a Disney plug, but it is funny how universal truths can make their way into almost anything. I have to tell you how the movie *Pocahontas* connected a role of the Holy Spirit for me. My daughter went through a phase where she was totally into this Native American princess. She had the costume and we even went to the original Jamestown that year and walked where the real Pocahontas had walked. One time I was watching the movie with her and I had this "aha moment." His Spirit revealed something I had been wondering about, through a Disney movie.

Below is the passage I had been mulling over in my head. Now a quick back story, this verse comes from the conversation Jesus and Nicodemus had, involving the ever-famous John 3:16. But that is not the verse I was pondering. Jesus makes this statement about people born of the Spirit of God.

> *The wind blows wherever it pleases. You hear its sound, but you cannot tell where it comes from or where it is going. So it is with everyone born of the Spirit.*
>
> (John 3:8, NIV)

I read this and thought, "What in the world is that even talking about?" I asked God about it, and not long after, during a *Pocahontas* marathon, *BOOM*. I got my answer.

In the story, Pocahontas's dad is searching for her and the village elder says, "You know Pocahontas, she has her mother's spirit. She goes wherever the wind takes her."[26]

Right then, the lightbulb turned on and the meaning of the verse was suddenly illuminated.

People who are born of the Spirit go where He "blows" them. We follow where He leads. We don't always know where we are heading, we just trust the One who does. When being led by God's Spirit, we transfer control. This is a tough one. We feel safe when we're in charge. But if we are to be led by the Holy Spirit of God, we have to be willing to trust that the Lord knows what He is doing and consent to follow His leading.

Even if it is scary.

Even if the way seems unclear.

Even if it seems impossible.

Even if we don't think we are strong enough.

We can follow the leading of God's Spirit when we believe that He is bigger than all of our doubts, stronger than our enemy, and going with us.

FRUIT OF THE UNION

Every Christmas my husband can't wait to take a bite of his favorite seasonal dessert: Fruit Cake. In my opinion, that atrocity should not be called a cake. I mean, where is the frosting, or at least some kind of glaze?! Plus, cake tastes amazing. And fruit cake... just doesn't. I don't know if I haven't had a good sampling, but it reminds me of licorice (which in my opinion is unworthy to be called candy) and bad tasting gummies, ruining a perfectly good white cake. But still, he loves it. Andrew thinks it is delicious. So, out of the love of my heart, I'll pick him up one to surprise him, to the detriment of my grocery budget. But hey, sacrifices must be made if a marriage is going to work, ha!

Now, apple pie, banana bread, berry cobblers—all desserts comprised of actual fruit—have it going on. I support and consume those desserts. There is a right way and a wrong way to create a dessert from fruit, am I right? And when all the correct ingredients are present it is a culinary masterpiece. *Come on somebody?!* Did I mention I am foodie? And dessert—well it is my favorite kind of food.

Did you know God calls us His masterpiece? And he wants us comprised of fruit, too. When we follow the leading of the Holy Spirit of God, His fruit is present, dripping from our soul and pouring out into a world that desperately needs a taste of that kind of fruit.

But the Holy Spirit produces this kind of fruit in

*our lives: love, joy, peace, patience, kindness,
goodness, faithfulness, gentleness, and self-
control. There is no law against these things!*
(Galatians 5:22-23)

A healthy, thriving tree produces loads of delicious tasting fruit, as should a follower of Christ. But often we make the fruit our focus, instead of simply focusing on being in tune with God's Spirit. We think we've got to love more, be more patient, be more faithful... these are good things, but producing this fruit isn't your job, it is His. *But the Holy Spirit produces this kind of fruit*, the verse says. Our goal is to know Him, do as He leads, walk in step with Him, and be filled with Him; the byproduct of that relation-ship is lasting fruit.

I love what evangelist Billy Graham shares about the fruit in a believer's life.

It is interesting that the Bible talks of the fruit of the Spirit rather than the fruits. A tree may bear many apples, but all come from the same tree. In the same way, the Holy Spirit is the source of all fruit in our lives. Put in simplest terms, the Bible tells us we need the Spirit to bring fruit into our lives because we cannot produce godliness apart from the Spirit.[27]

For a long time I strived to have these fruits present in my life, all the while skipping over the get-to-know-the-

Holy-Spirit part. We can't love, be patient, or kind in our own strength for very long. In our own power these attributes, this list of fruit, is just impossible to possess constantly—trust me I've tried—unsuccessfully I might add. To be a person flowing in the gifts of the Spirit we must not go at it alone. We have a helper.

'Not by might nor by power, but by my Spirit,'
says the LORD Almighty.
(Zechariah 4:6b, NIV)

Throughout the Bible, we see a God who wants to be present in our life. He wants to help us accomplish amazing things TOGETHER. What if we shifted our energy and time from working on ourselves to working on a life focused on following as His Spirit leads? As we follow and grow closer to Him, the Spirit will supernaturally produce fruit in our lives.

GO WITH THE FLOW

When I was in high school, I used to perform in talent shows yearly with my youth group "step team." Every year at summer camp we did a step routine. The music was rockin' and our feet were stompin'. (I'm fairly sure this little factoid will surprise a few of my friends as they learn about of the secret hobby of my past.) The crowd always went nuts because it was so different than the skits and solos the other contestants were doing. It was so fun and those few moments on stage were electric. The crowd always enjoyed it on performance night, but what they had not seen was all the practice that went into perfecting our routine.

For hours and hours we rehearsed the moves over and over, getting everything just right. If anyone was off it messed up the rhythm of the whole group. And when this happened we helped each other out, came alongside, and worked together until everyone was in unison. The end product of all our hard work was magnificent. Once we got plugged into the rhythm, the performance was dynamic.

God has given us His Spirit to lead us and empower us to minister to others. He wants us to plug into the rhythm of what His Spirit is doing and accomplish great things together. God wants us to know Him as the Spirit and be tuned into the flow of where He leads. This is true for us personally, but also for the body of Jesus Christ as a whole. Can you imagine if we all tapped into the leading of the Spirit of God and all of our hearts and purposes aligned? What a magnificent and world changing people we would be! We, as sons and daughters of the Most High, all flowing with God would be a bright shining light. The darkness would flee and that kind of light would illuminate the world.

You are the light of the world—like a city on a hilltop that cannot be hidden.
(Matthew 5:14)

In Revelation, John writes about a future city. A city where God is central and Jesus is enthroned and the living water of the Holy Spirit is running down the center of the city. Let's look at this passage and pay attention to what is growing on the banks of the river. What is plugged into the water of life?

> *Then the angel showed me a river with the water of life, clear as crystal, flowing from the throne of God and of the Lamb. It flowed down the center of the main street. On each side of the river grew a tree of life, bearing twelve crops of fruit, with a fresh crop each month. The leaves were used for medicine to heal the nations.*
> (Revelation 22:1-2)

Trees. Strong, thriving, fruit-yielding trees. There are trees of life growing on either side of the river. Life-giving, health-bringing, vibrant trees are growing and ministering to the nations of the world. Could these be us? Is it possible that these trees represent believers who are plugged into the river of water of life? A person who knows God as Father, Son, and Spirit and has Him enthroned in their heart and walking in step with all that He is doing?

Let's be THOSE trees. Let's be THAT city.

Let's know God as Spirit and stay continually connecting and flowing with the river of life. Let's be so full of the water of the Holy Spirit that when we meet someone who is thirsty, we can pour out and point them to the true source of our living water.

A strong tree needs a good source of water to thrive, and boy, do we have one.

> *But blessed is the man who trusts me, GOD, the woman who sticks with GOD. They're like trees replanted in Eden, putting down roots near the rivers—Never a worry through the hottest of summers, never dropping a leaf, Serene and calm through droughts, bearing fresh fruit every season.*
> (Jeremiah 17:7-8, MSG)

When we connect with God who is Spirit, our souls come alive and our roots go deep and soak up His refreshing, life-giving water. This is what our souls thirst for. I think people sometimes shy away from the things of the Spirit, because He seems mysterious and unpredictable. But without being acquainted with the third person of the Trinity, we cannot fully connect with God and we're missing out on the full life that is available to us.

> *There will be swarms of living things wherever the water of this river flows. Fish will abound in the Dead Sea, for its waters will become fresh. Life will flourish wherever this water flows.*
> (Ezekie 47:9)

This is such a beautiful picture of what the Holy Spirit does. Whatever the river of the Spirit touches, wherever it goes it brings life. It revives. Whatever is flowing in sync with the Holy Spirit of God is alive and flourishing.

You can put a seed in the most fertile ground on the planet, and position it to receive the perfect amount of sunlight, but it will never grow into the tree it is meant to be without being watered. It will stay there, waiting to come alive. Water is essential for abundant growth, just as the right nutrient-rich soil and adequate sunlight is needed. Not one element can be neglected. We need to be people who are connected to and open to the leading of the Spirit.

God the Spirit *gives* us what we need, when we need it, *takes* us where we are supposed to go, and *fills* our hearts with passion and fire for the purpose God has planned for us. To reach our fullest potential and live a life overflowing with His power, we need to be one with the Holy Spirit.

HE IS MY SUPPLY & SOURCE OF LIFE
I AM SUSTAINED BY THE HOLY SPIRIT.

DIGGING DEEPER

Listen to "Here Again," by Elevation Worship.

Read Galatians 5:25.

1. Are there any fears that hold you back from going where the Spirit leads? What are they?

2. How would your willingness to submit to the Holy Spirit's nudgings change if you remained confident in the power of God in every situation?

3. In what ways can you intentionally pursue deeper connection with the Holy Spirit in your life?

Conclusion

Just like trees—when rooted in good soil, supplied with ample water and adequate sunlight— thrive, we too grow stronger, going from strength to strength as we know our God more. The more balanced we are in pursuing a deeper connection to Him as Father, Son, and Spirit—all three sides of the trinity—the brighter the fire in our hearts burn for Him and His cause. Typically fire and plants don't mix too well, in fact Smokey the Bear would have a lot to say about bringing a flame around a forest of trees. But there is one time a holy flame collided with a bush and the result was pretty memorable.

> *There the angel of the LORD appeared to him in flames of fire from within a bush. Moses saw that though the bush was on fire it did not burn up. So Moses thought, "I will go over and see this strange sight—why the bush does not burn*

up." When the LORD saw that he had gone over to look, God called to him from within the bush, "Moses! Moses!" And Moses said, "Here I am!"

(Exodus 3:2-4, NIV)

God was in the bush, God was in the fire, and God was the flame. As we're connected to: God the Father—His love pours out of us; the Son—we shine His light; the Spirit—life is connected to the source and our hearts are set ablaze, turning us into the children of God that the world needs us to be. God is our love, God is our light, God is our life, and He is the fire in our veins.

When we are totally rooted in the love of Father God, restored in the light of all our Savior is and has done for us, and invigorated by being led and walking every day in friendship with the Spirit of God, we are fully ourselves. Completely connected, loved, united, in awe of Him, this is how it is meant to be.

Our God is awe-some. He's always wanted us plugged into Him as the source of all life, so we can grow into these living trees. This unity with God frees us to love and serve others. Being one with Him enables us to show others the way to meet the God who loves them, the Savior who came for them, the Spirit who's ready to help them. It is easy to tell people about someone you know and spend time with.

As a tree grows strong when the right elements are

present, so we too are strengthened as we become one with our God, the Awesome One. He manifests in three ways, yet He is one. As believers who want to live an explosive life—full of love, light, and purpose—we need to know God as Father, Son, and Spirit more. As we discover who He is, we find out who we truly are. Loved. Righteous. Powerful. We need to be united with The Awesome One so that we can change the world.

I PRAY THAT THEY WILL ALL BE ONE, JUST AS YOU AND I ARE ONE—AS YOU ARE IN ME, FATHER, AND I AM IN YOU. AND MAY THEY BE IN US SO THAT THE WORLD WILL BELIEVE YOU SENT ME
—JESUS
JOHN 17:21

ACKNOWLEDGEMENTS

I want to take time to thank everyone who played a part in this book coming to fruition—because without their much-needed support, you would not be reading these words.

To God—the treasure of my life. Thank you for trusting me with this message. You believed in me first. Your unconditional love and relentless grace has made me the woman who I am, and without your guiding voice and faithful provision, none of this would be possible. To you be ALL glory and praise.

To Andrew—my love, soul mate, and best friend. Thank you for believing in me—especially on those days I didn't believe in myself. Your "northern boldness" has rubbed off on me, giving me the confidence I needed to share these truths. You lead and protect our family faithfully and have taught me how to forgive everyone, always. Our kids are pretty lucky to have such a fun, generous, Christ-like dad. Love you babe. Also, thanks for letting me sneak away to the coffee shop on the regular so I could finish this project.

To Drew, Emma, and Jack—my creative, full-of-life, amazing kids. Thank you for frequently telling me, "You're the best mom ever." Some days when I feel like I've dropped the ball, those words mean the world to me. I'm so grateful God chose me to be your mama. Thank you for encouraging me, for the laughs, and for all the interesting stories (that just keep on coming)! You keep me smiling. God has his hand on each of you in a special way and it is my great joy to get a front row seat to watch how He uses you.

To my mama—thank you for showing me what it looks like to be in God's word every day, and for modeling a servant's heart. You've inspired me in ways you'll never know. You have always supported and been proud of me, and that has brought so much courage to my heart.

To my daddy—thank you for instilling in me a love of music and worship of God, even if the musical gene did skip over me! You still taught me to appreciate it. You've always believed bigger for me than I can even imagine. Thanks for teaching me to be a dreamer.

To Bud and Glenida—thank you for treating me as one of

your own. You have always made me feel a part of the family, you raised a wonderful son to be my husband, and the way you love my kids is so evident. You model sacrifice and diligence, and through adversity, you look for the silver lining, and somehow find a way to still encourage others.

To my Grandpas, Grandmas, and family members — thank you for praying for me throughout my whole life; your faithfulness played a part in the writing and publishing of this book. I'm grateful!

To Pastors Jason and Nicole Rollin — thank you for truly caring for me and my family. Your love and support gave us wings to fly. You both are true trail blazers, servant-leaders, and love with your whole heart. Your faithfulness is an inspiration and words can't express what your friendship, leadership, and support means to me. Thank you for believing in and always dreaming with me! Nicole, if I could meet you for coffee and a donut every day and dream together, I would!

To Pastor Steven and Holly Furtick — thank you for mentoring me from afar. God has used you both to build my faith, help me regain confidence, and lead with integrity, as you both do. Thank you for being faithful in walking out the vision of Elevation Church, as it is changing lives all over the world, including my own.

To Terry and Ellen Bruce, Matt and Dana Beasley, and the entire Elevation Uptown staff—thank you for welcoming us into your family. I am thankful for your leadership and direction, and for always calling me up, to see myself the way God does and see others through the lens of love and grace. I'm grateful to serve Charlotte with you.

To Dianne Wyper—thank you for being my constant friend who offers encouragement, advice, and laughs when they are most needed. Thanks for being a friend who I can dream big with, and for all the late night—wait who am I kidding—ALL day coffee conversations. I love talking Jesus, the goodness of God, and righteousness with you. You are my conference-going, coffee-loving, soul sister and I'm grateful God crossed our paths.

To Stacey Patterson—thank you for being a great friend and encourager for almost my whole life. You've always been a voice of wisdom and source of laughter. We've grown up together, and this means you know the good, the bad, and the ugly, and you still want to hang around me; that is saying something. I am grateful God brought us back together after all these years and it has been a true joy watching you put into practice everything in this book. Your freedom says it all. I love and treasure you both and words cannot express how thankful I am to have you as a constant source of encouragement.

To the UNITED HOUSE team—thank you, every single one of you. Without your input, expertise, and encouragement this book would have never happened. You have truly become a family to me, and I am honored to partner with you and God on this amazing journey of making people's dreams come true.

To Logan Lewis—thank you for all the laughs as we worked through this book, and others together. You seriously add the magic with your gift. Without your help, I would not sound nearly as smart or witty. I'm grateful for all the time you spent on getting this book "just right."

To Charity Walkowski—thank you for liking me! I know I say that to you all the time, but it is such a special treasure to have someone who really likes you for you, and you do. From the first time I had you over to coffee at my house, I knew we would be the best of friends! Thank you for adding fuel to the flames of my dreams, and not only that, you joined me in the adventure! I appreciate all that you've done for UNITED HOUSE, but more importantly all the ways you support me. Love you to pieces.

To Natasha Tubbs—thank you for your consistent support
my vision. You have been a needed peer and
alked this book-publishing journey. I am grate-
ou have done for us at UNITED HOUSE.

To Caitlyn Spencer, Kalli Drake, Cara Lawson, and Julia Amting—thank you for all the additions, honest feedback, and creativity you brought to this book. You all have a gift! I'm grateful that God brought each of you to the team just as this project was needing input. Caitlyn, I'll always be grateful for the day you asked how you could be a part of UNITED HOUSE. #answertoprayer (I also love that you are a fellow coffee snob—my sister!)

To Kelly Wentz and *THE AWESOME ONE* Book Launch Team—thank you for helping me to stay organized, for brainstorming ideas with me, and for being some of the first readers and cheerleaders for *THE AWESOME ONE*. Your feedback and input gave me the energy support to get this book out to the world! I could not have trusted the sharing of this message with a greater community of friends.

To Christina Martinico—thank you for being my first Elevation Church friend. I can't believe I met you on day one at Elevation Uptown. It was pretty ironic that my first NC friend after returning from living 14 years in Michigan was from Michigan, and even came from the church Andrew and I met at. Only God. Thank you for including and inviting me into your group. That invitation led to a community where I could belong. You'll never know how much your love impacted me—a girl who felt a little lost in a new church and missing all my friends back home. I'm forever grateful!

To my Soul Sisters eGroup (Christina, Laura, Ro, Jenn, Kelly, Jennifer, Angela, Natalie, Megan, Liz, Becky, Isabel, Jessica, Morgan, Sandy, Sue, Suzy, and Stacey)—thank you for allowing me to be a part of the gang and giving me the spiritual support I needed to finish this project. You gals accepted me and prayed for me from day one, and the way you serve Charlotte has been nothing short of life-changing for me. Angela and Natalie, serving at Dove's Nest with you (and Stacey) has been one of the highlights of my move back to Charlotte. Love laughing and serving with you!

To Kim Beecham and Casey Patterson—thank you for being life-long friends who have always believed in my gift. Kim, I'll never forget the day you said, "You should write a book one day." It was the encouragement that I needed to actually start. Thank you for sticking with me through thick and thin.

To Linda Aarni, Jenny Brown, Melissa Neal, Jessica Prukner, Jenna Schneider, Jessica Russel, Casey Patterson, and Holly Thomson—thank you for being my good friends who I know I can call in an instant to stand in prayer with me. You all are inspire me to be a better wife, mom, business owner, writer, and speaker. Your lives have impacted me in one way or another, and I am so grateful to call you friends and for your continual support and prayers. Your encouragement got me here, and you have ⬚⬚⬚ know God more.

To every friend and encourager—thank you to everyone whoever called me friend, believed in the plans God had for me, and spoke life into my dream of writing a book one day. Your words went a long way, and not only did they lead to me writing a book, but enabled me to help others write and publish their stories too. I'm grateful!

NOTES

1. Packer, J. I. *Knowing God,* 33. Westmont, IL: InterVarsity Press, 1993.

2. Chan, Francis. *Forgotten God,* 20-21. Colorado Springs, CO: David C. Cook, 2009.

3. Liebscher, Banning. *Rooted: The hidden places where God develops you,* 43. Colorado Springs, CO: WaterBrook, 2016.

4. Einstein, Albert. "Albert Einstein Quotes." BrainyQuotes, Accessed January 15, 2018. https://www.brainyquote.com/quotes/albert_einstein_148778.

5. Smith, Judah. *How's Your Soul?,* 167. Nashville, TN: Nelson Books, 2016.

6. Wilkerson, Jr., Rich. *Sandcastle Kings: Meeting Jesus in a spiritually bankrupt world,*

151-152. Nashville, TN: Nelson Books, 2015.

7. Moody, D. L. *The life of Dwight L. Moody*, 40. London, England: Morgan and Scott, 1900.

8. Prince Joseph, *The Power of Right Believing*, 49. New York, NY: FaithWords, 2013.

9. Eldredge, Stasi. *Captivating: Unveiling the mystery of a woman's soul*, 96. Nashville, TN: Thomas Nelson, 2010.

10. Smith, Judah. *LIFE IS _____.: God's illogical love will change your existence*, 1. Nashville, TN: Nelson Books, 2015.

11. Houston, Brian. *Live Love Lead*, 55. New York, NY: FaithWords, 2015.

12. Connolly, Jess. *Wild and Free*, 80. Grand Rapids, MI: Zondervan, 2016.

13. Caine, Christine. *UNDAUNTED:Daring to do what God calls you to do*, 114. Grand Rapids: MI, 2012.

14. Liebscher, Banning. *JESUS CULTURE: Calling a generation to revival*, 117. Shippensburg, PA: Destiny Image Publishers Inc., 2015.

15. BibleHub. "Strong's Greek: 1343. (dikaiosuné)." Accessed March 20, 2018. http://biblehub.com/greek/1343.htm.

16. Gunn, Tricia. *Unveiling Jesus: Beholding Him in his amazing grace*, 96-97. Columbia, SC: Unveiling Jesus LLC, 2014.

17. Smith, Judah. *The Security of a Son;* 2018. Kirkland, WA. Churchome Message, April 22, 2018. https://churchome.org/message/the-security-of-a-son.

18. BibleHub. "Strong's Greek: 1344. (dikaioó)." Accessed March 28, 2018. https://biblehub.com/greek/1344.htm.

19. Prince, Joseph. *Destined To Reign*, 32-33. Tulsa, OK: Harrison House, 2010.

20. Furtick, Steven. *UNQUALIFIED: How God uses broken people to do big things*, 98. Colorado Springs, CO: Waterbrook Multnomah, 2016.

21. Wommack, Andrew. *GRACE, The Power of the Gospel*, 53, 67, 108-109. Tulsa, OK: Harrison House, 2007.

22. Lokulutu, Mercy. *Rooted in Christ;* 2018. Fayetteville, NC. Face 2 Face Women's Conference, March 16th, 2018.

23. Smith, Judah. *LIFE IS _____.: God's illogical love will change your existence,* 112-113. Nashville, TN: Nelson Books, 2015.

24. Bevere, John. *The Holy Spirit: An introduction*, 42. Palmer Lake, CO: Messenger International, 2013.

25. Bevere, John. *The Holy Spirit: An introduction*, 114. Palmer Lake, CO: Messenger International, 2013.

26. Gabriel, Mike and Goldberg, Eric, dir. Pocohantas. 1995; Burbank, CA: Walt Disney Pictures, 2000. DVD.

27. Graham, Billy. *The Holy Spirit: Activating God's power in your life*, 230. Nashville, TN: Thomas Nelson, 1988.

About The Author

Amber Olafsson is a wife, mama, author, speaker, and publisher who has a passion to see people connect with God and watch them step into their destiny as their world collides with His. She owns UNITED HOUSE Publishing where she helps others write and publish their world-changing stories.

Amber and her husband Andrew have been married since 2005, and together they co-founded United House Ministries. They have three amazing kids and live near Charlotte, NC. When she is not sipping a hot cup of craft coffee and reading a good book, she enjoys traveling and making memories with her family, gardening, decorating, and spending time at the feet of Jesus. You can get to know Amber more on Instagram @amber.olafsson and learn more about UNITED HOUSE Publishing at www.unitedhousepublishing.com.

94112667R10135

Made in the USA
Middletown, DE
17 October 2018